INNING

N THE

RAIN

ND OTHER LYRICS

ARCEL FEIGEL

LUSTRATIONS BY RUSSELL JONES

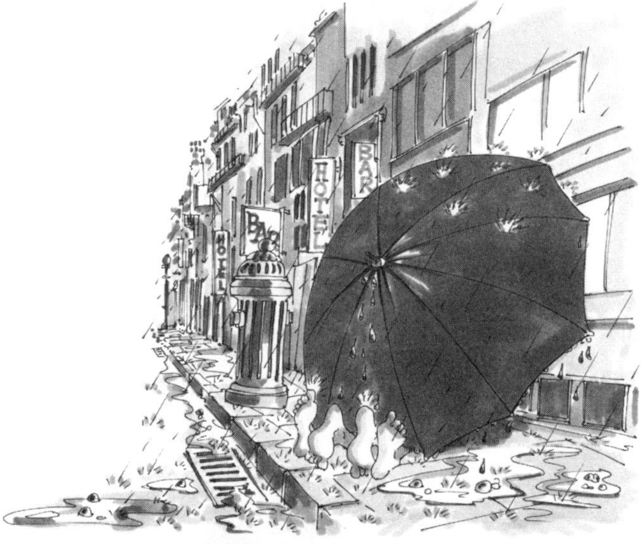

ULLER, BLOND & WHITE

With special thanks to Paul Ellis

First published in Great Britain in 1986 by Muller, Blond & White Limited,
55 Great Ormond Street, London WC1N 3HZ.

British Library Cataloguing in Publication Data

Feigel, Marcel
Sinning in the rain: and other lyrics
1. English wit and humor, Pictorial
I. Title
741.5-942 NC 1479

ISBN 0 584 11148 7

Printed and bound in Great Britain by
R.J. Acford Chichester

DEDICATED TO THE ONE I LOVE

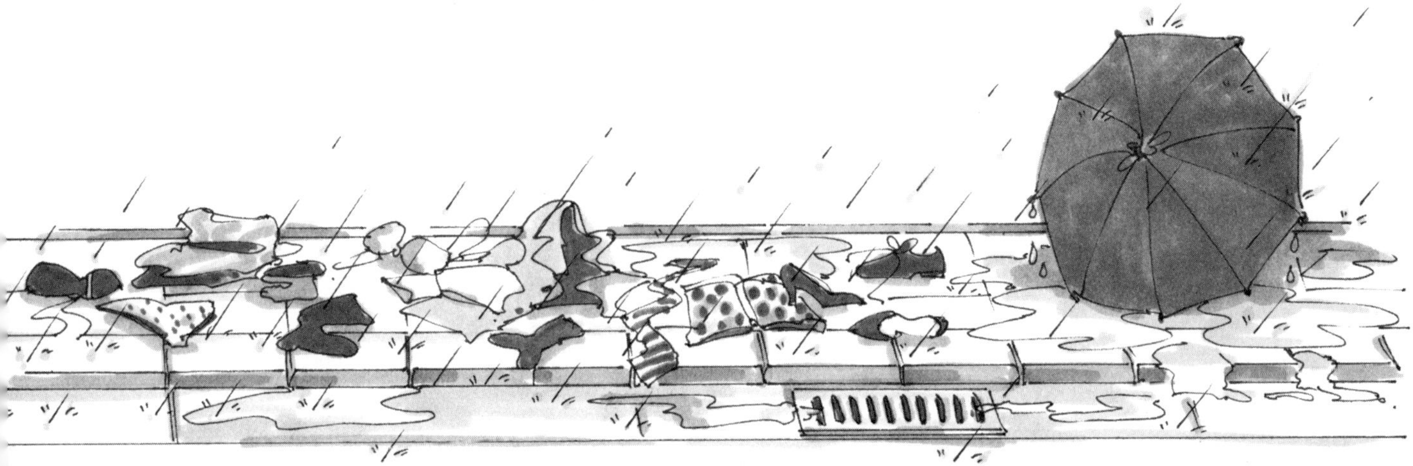

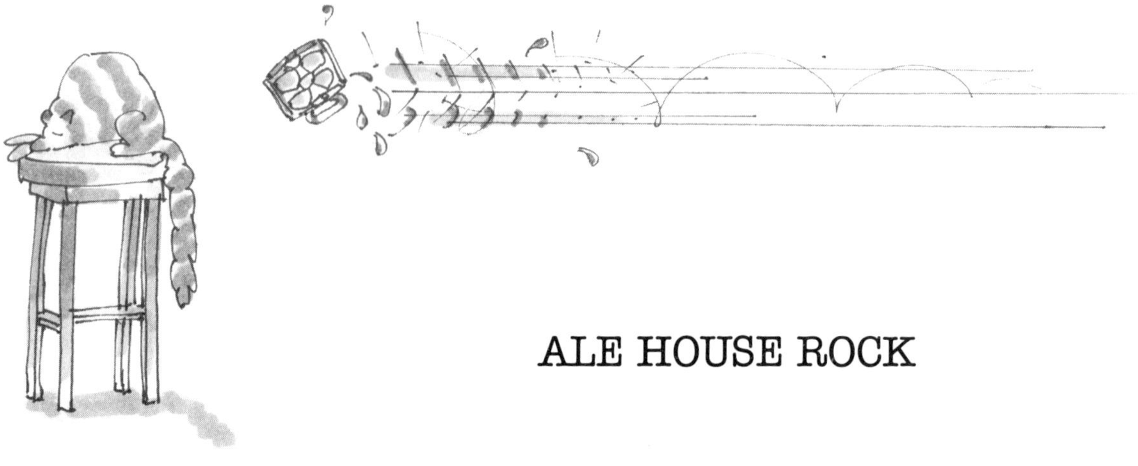

ALE HOUSE ROCK

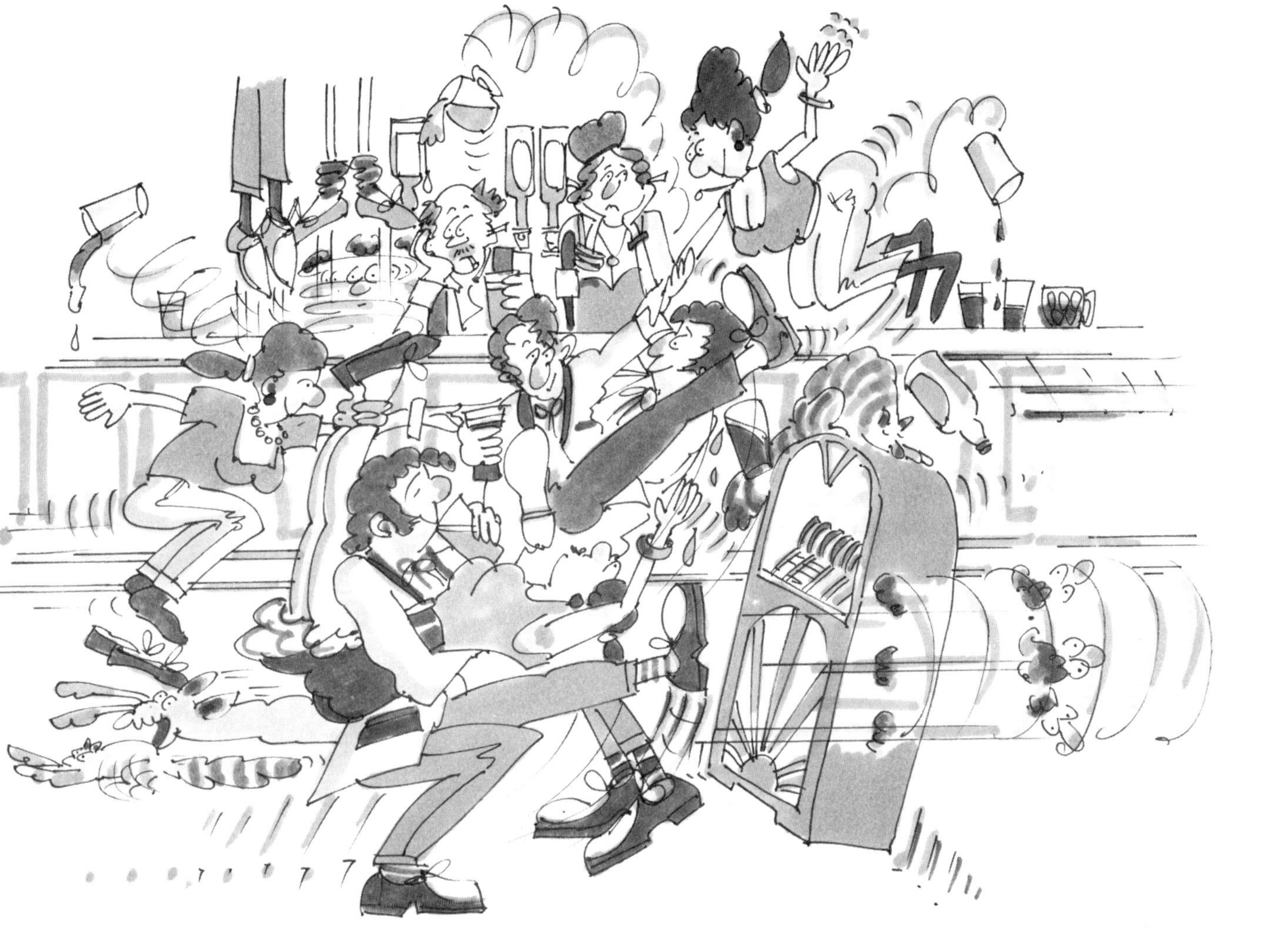

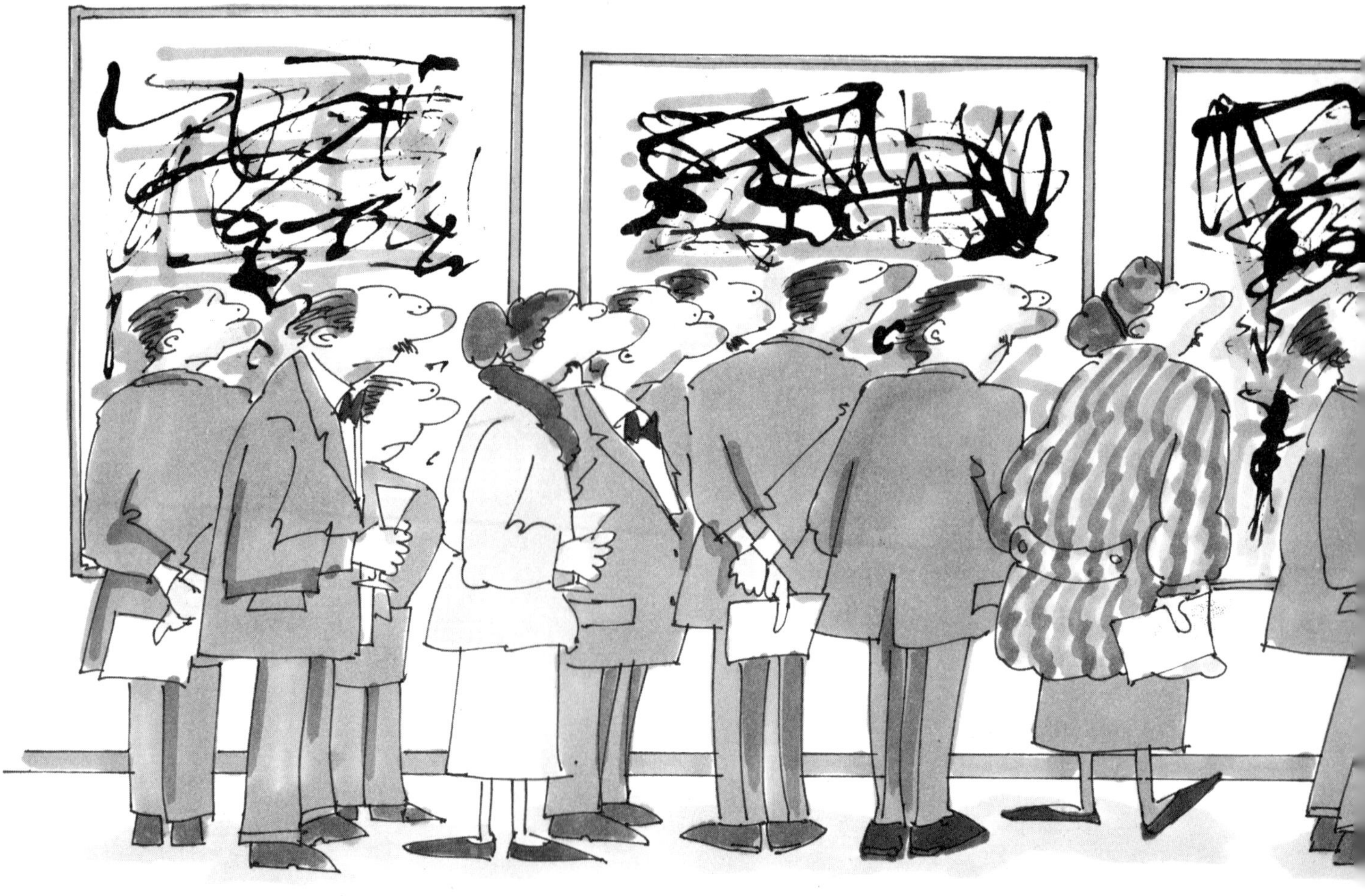

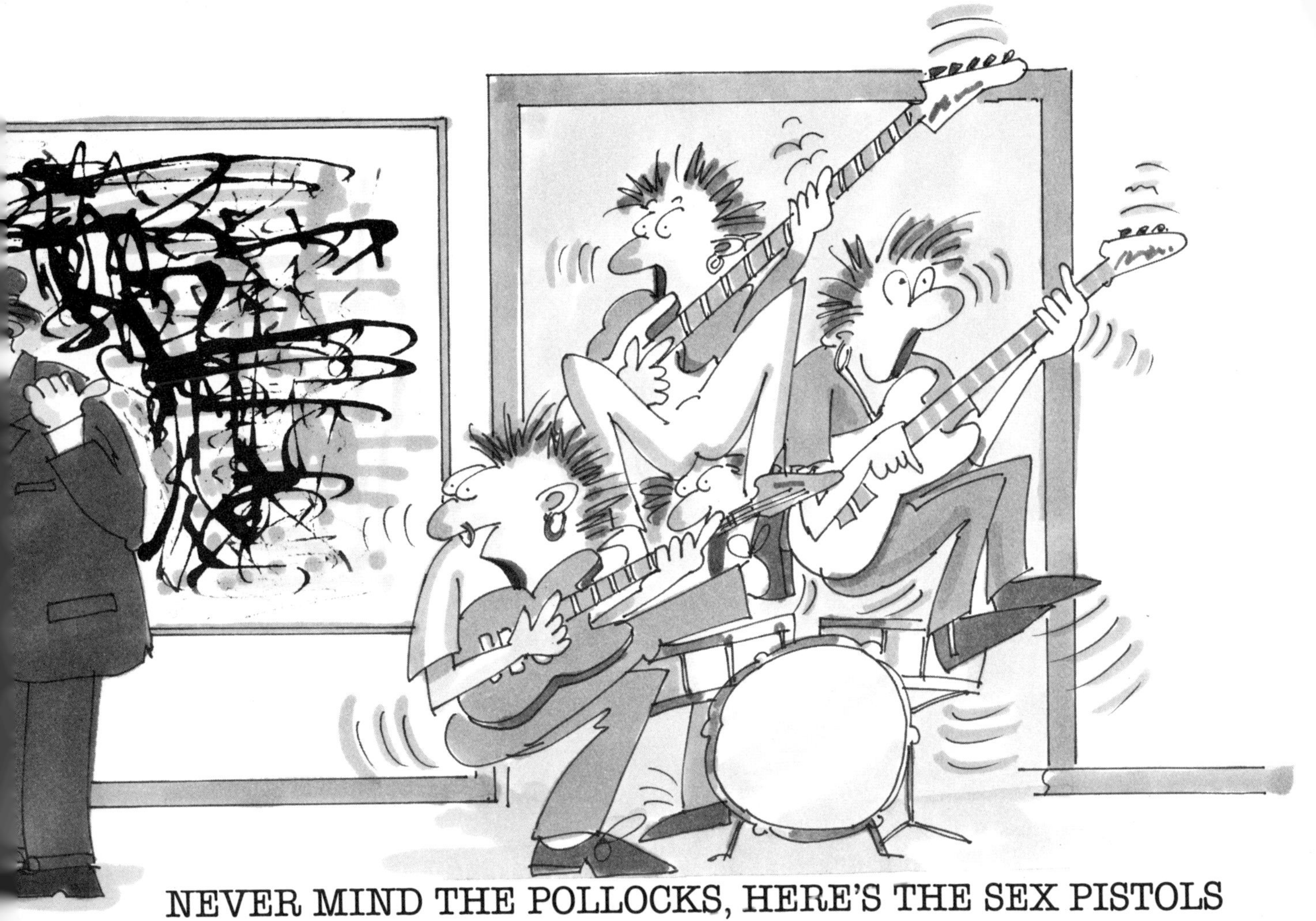

NEVER MIND THE POLLOCKS, HERE'S THE SEX PISTOLS

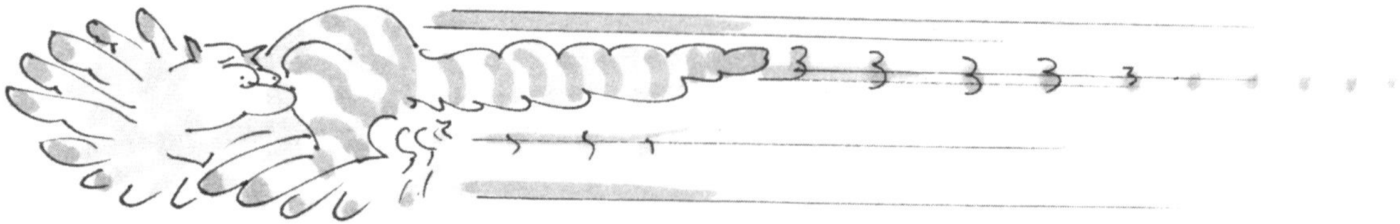

WHEREVER I HANG MY CAT THAT'S MY HOME

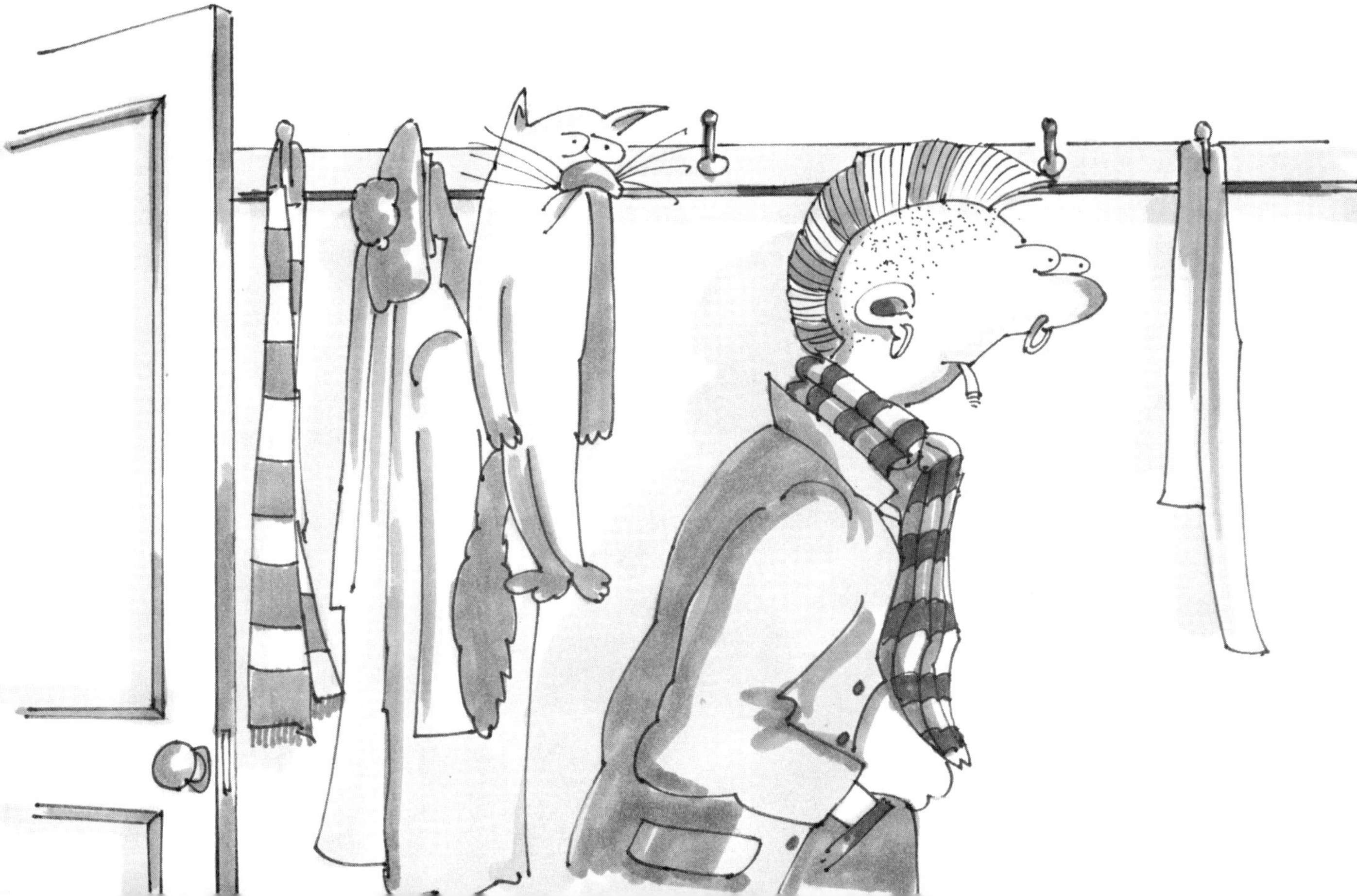

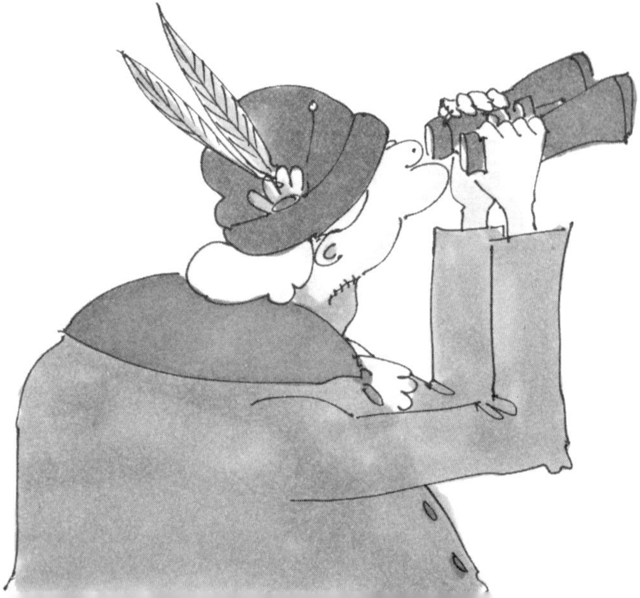

JUMPING MAC FLASH

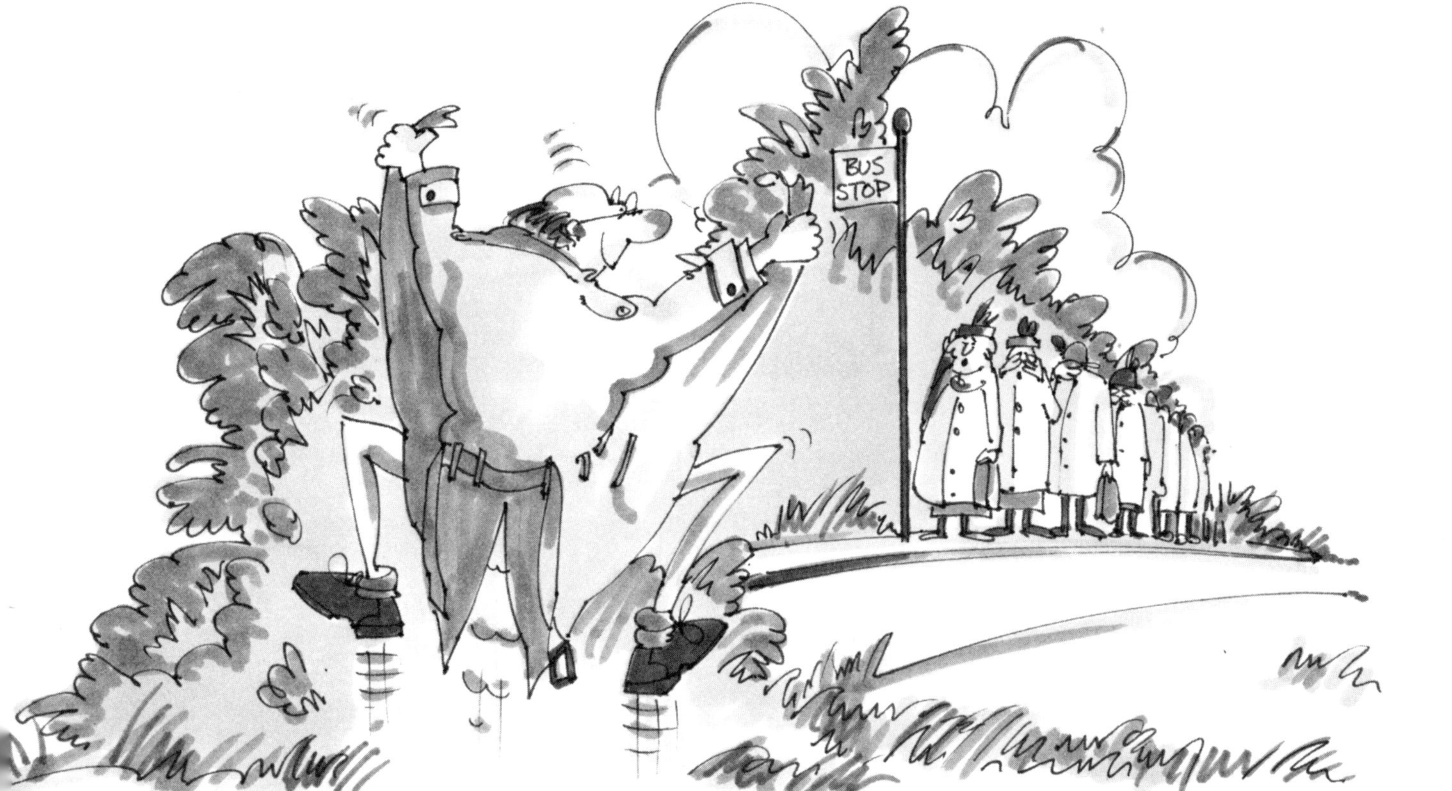
BUS
STOP

WE ARE FAILING, WE ARE FAILING

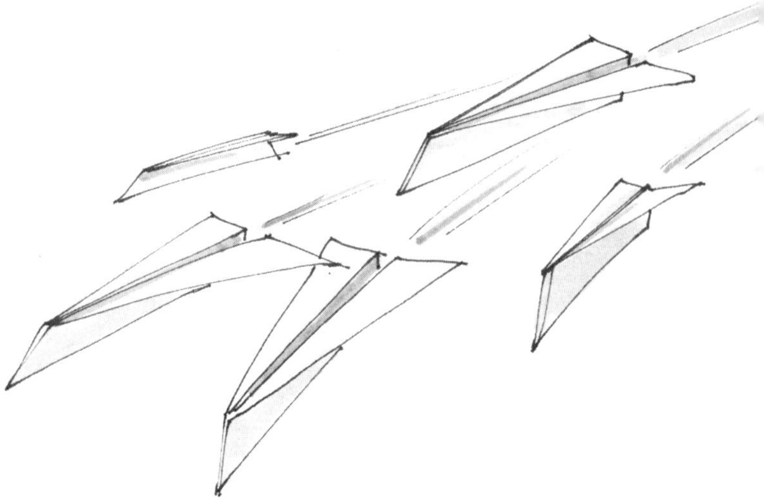

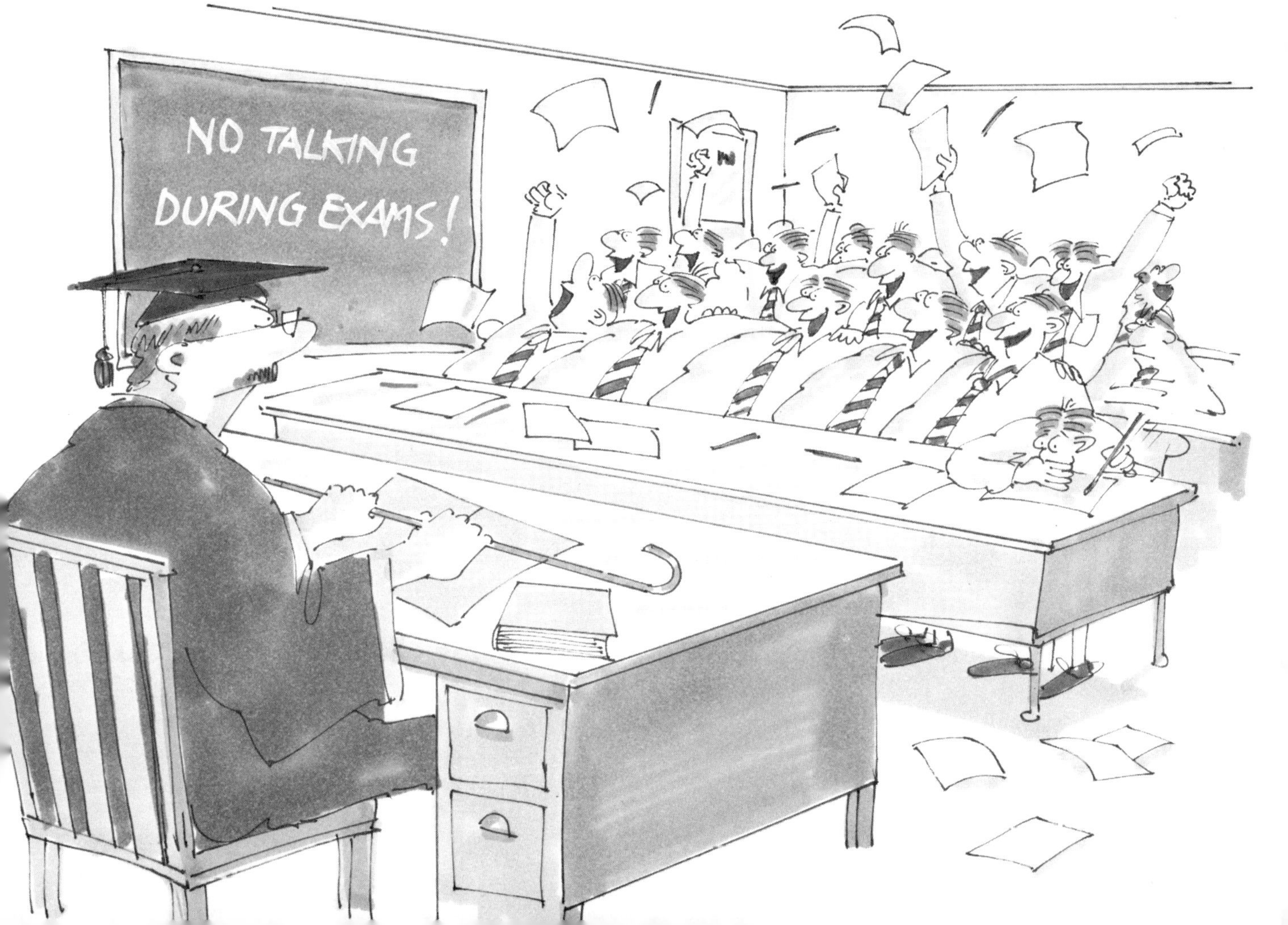
NO TALKING
DURING EXAMS!

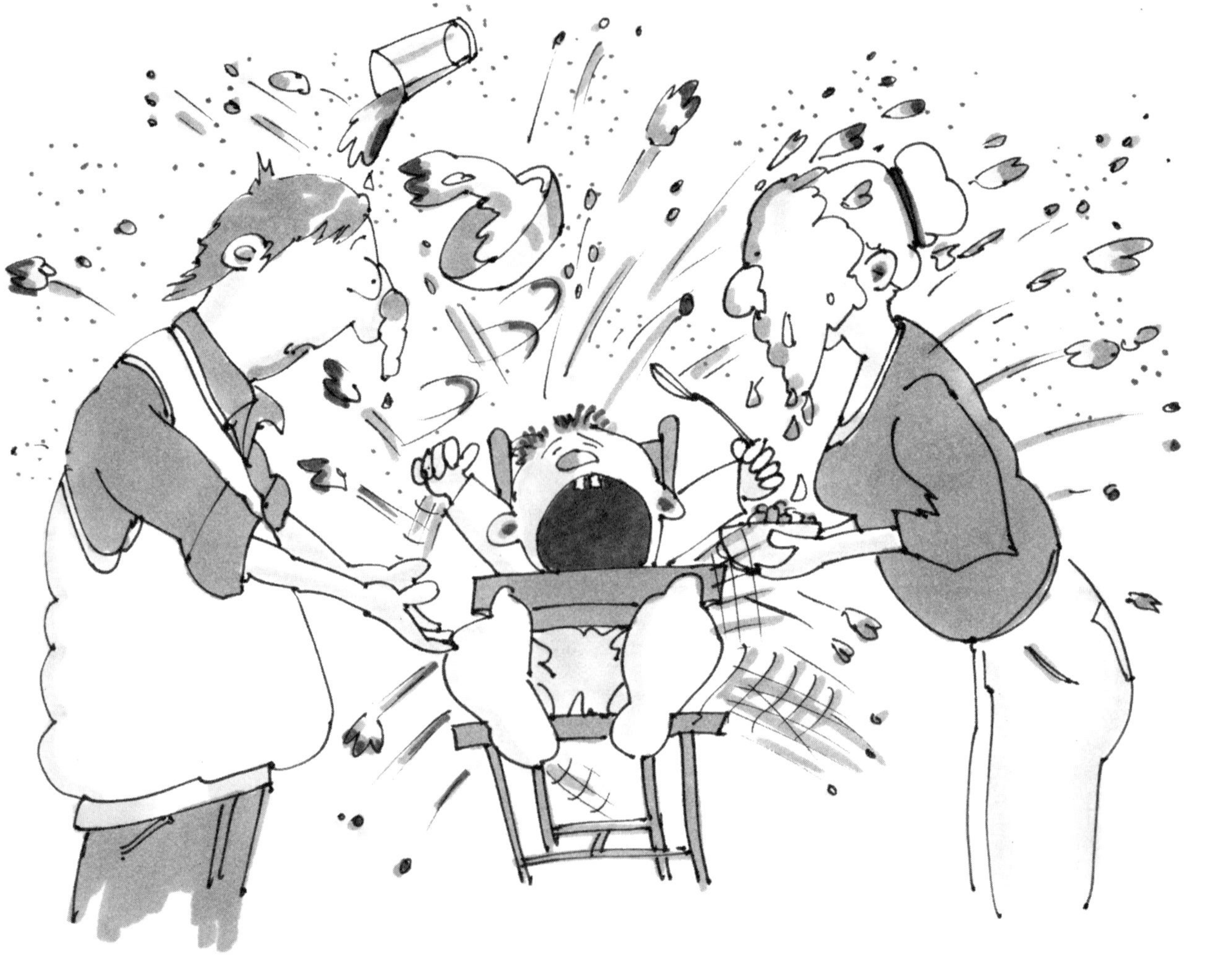

ALL WE ARE SAYING IS GIVE PEAS A CHANCE

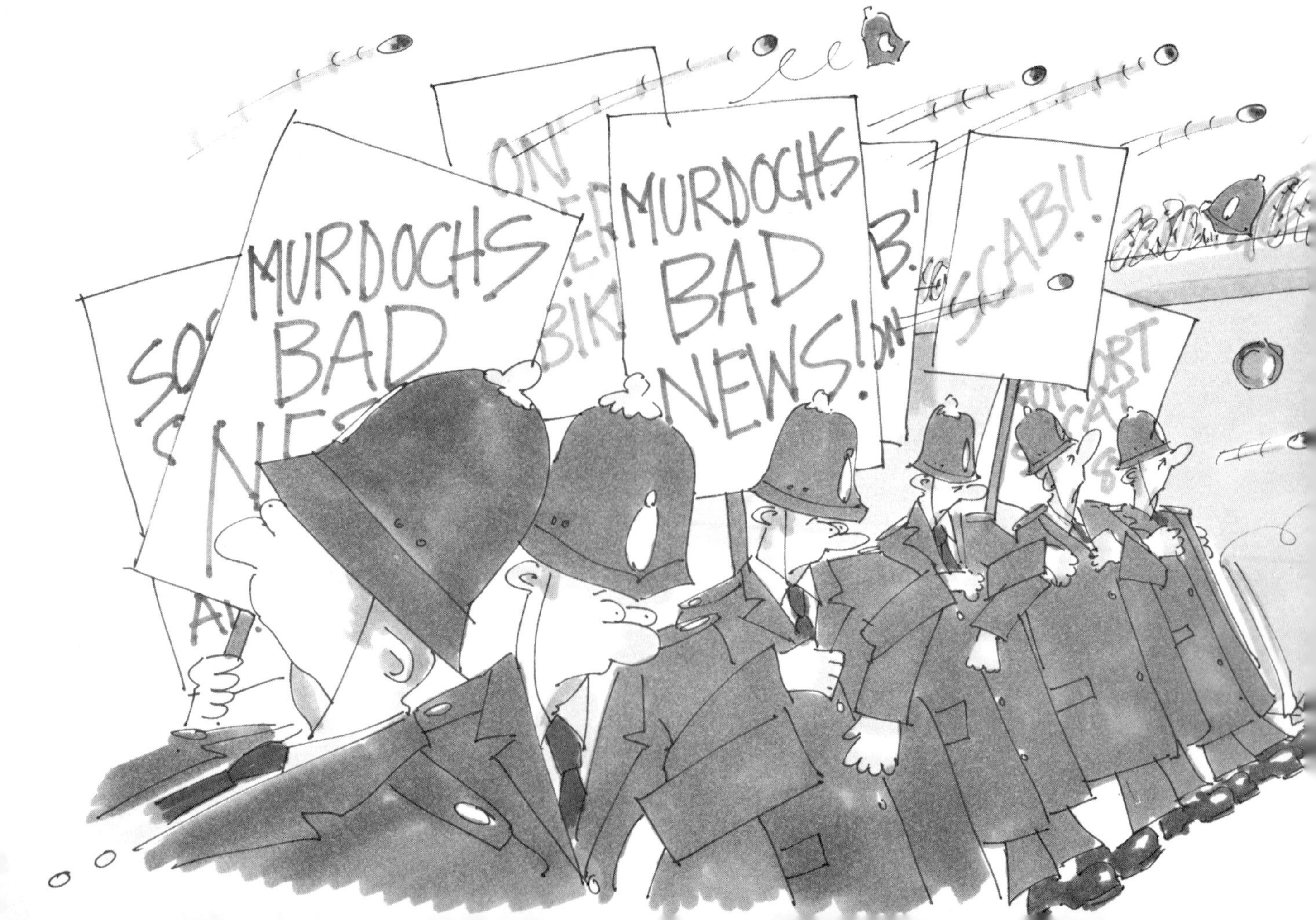
MURDOCHS
BAD
MURDOCHS
BAD
NEWS!!
SCAB!!

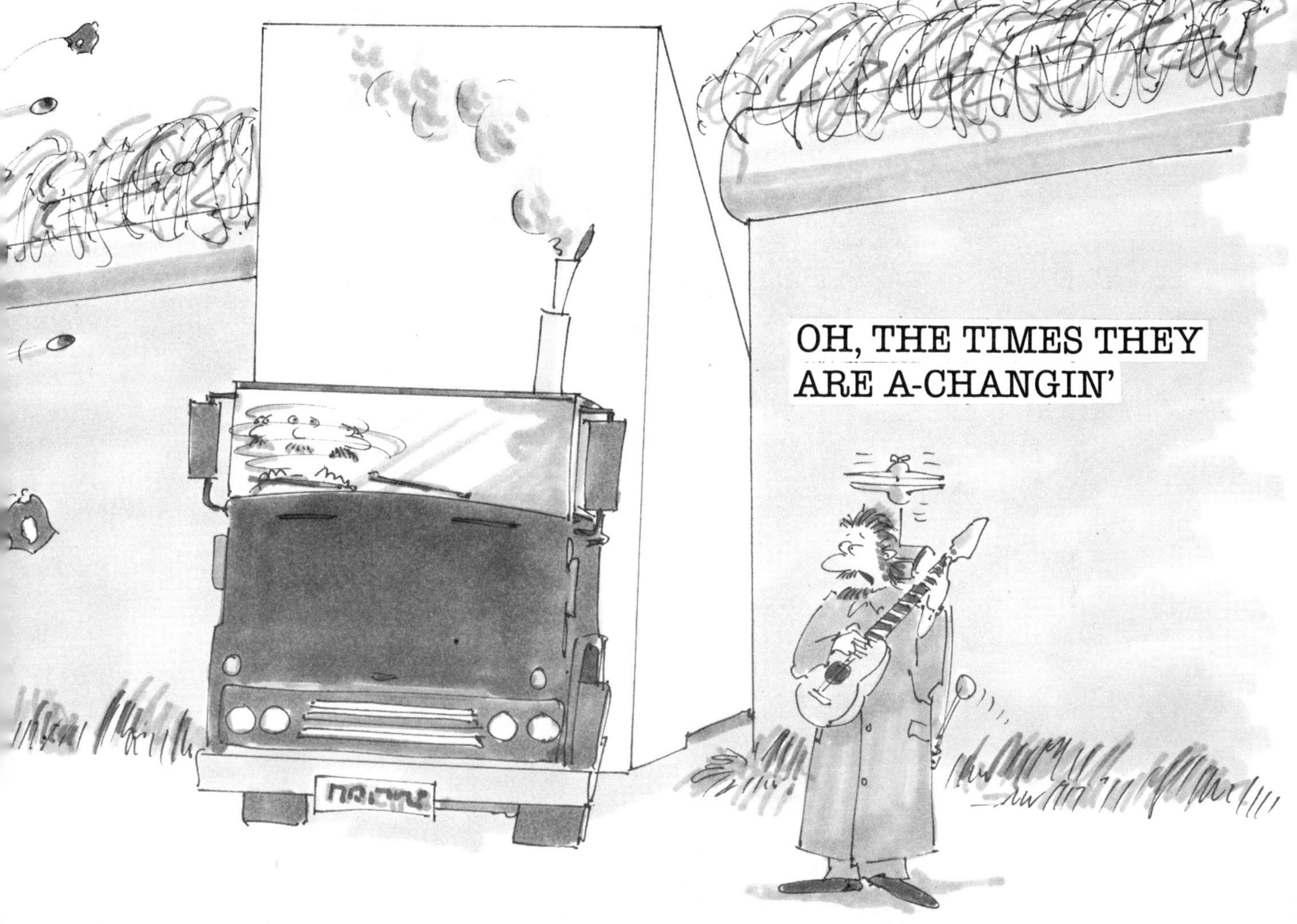
OH, THE TIMES THEY
ARE A-CHANGIN'

POOF THE MAGIC DRAGON

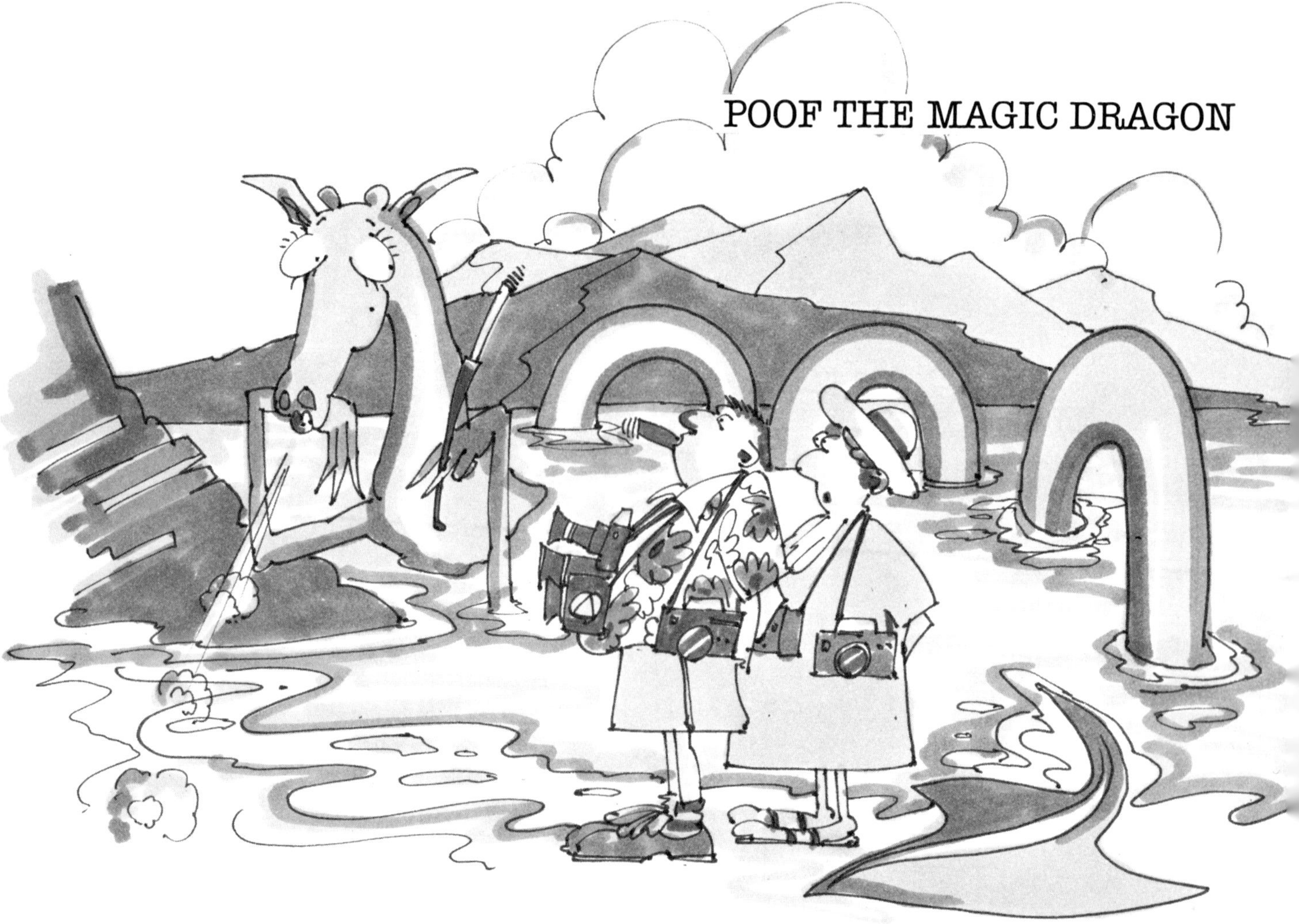

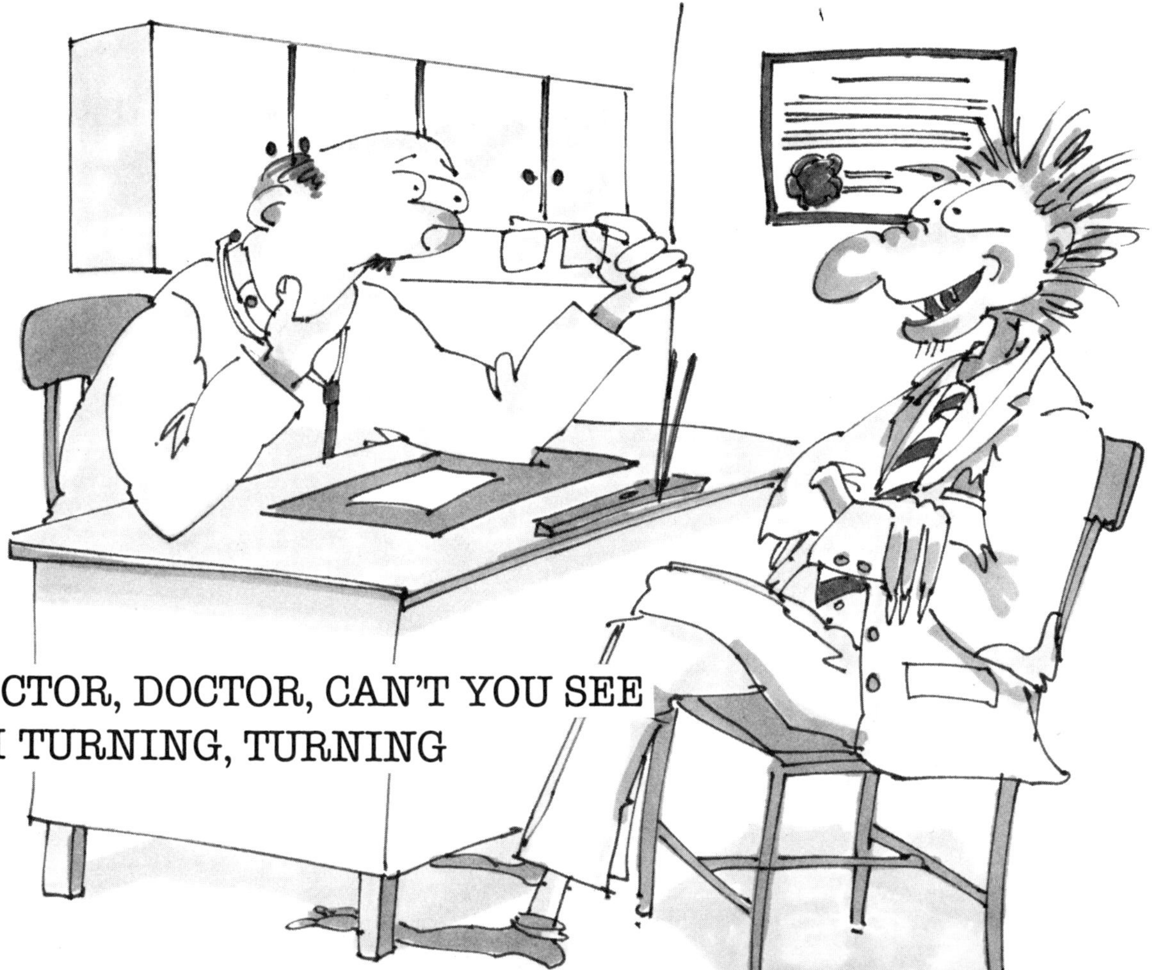

DOCTOR, DOCTOR, CAN'T YOU SEE
I'M TURNING, TURNING

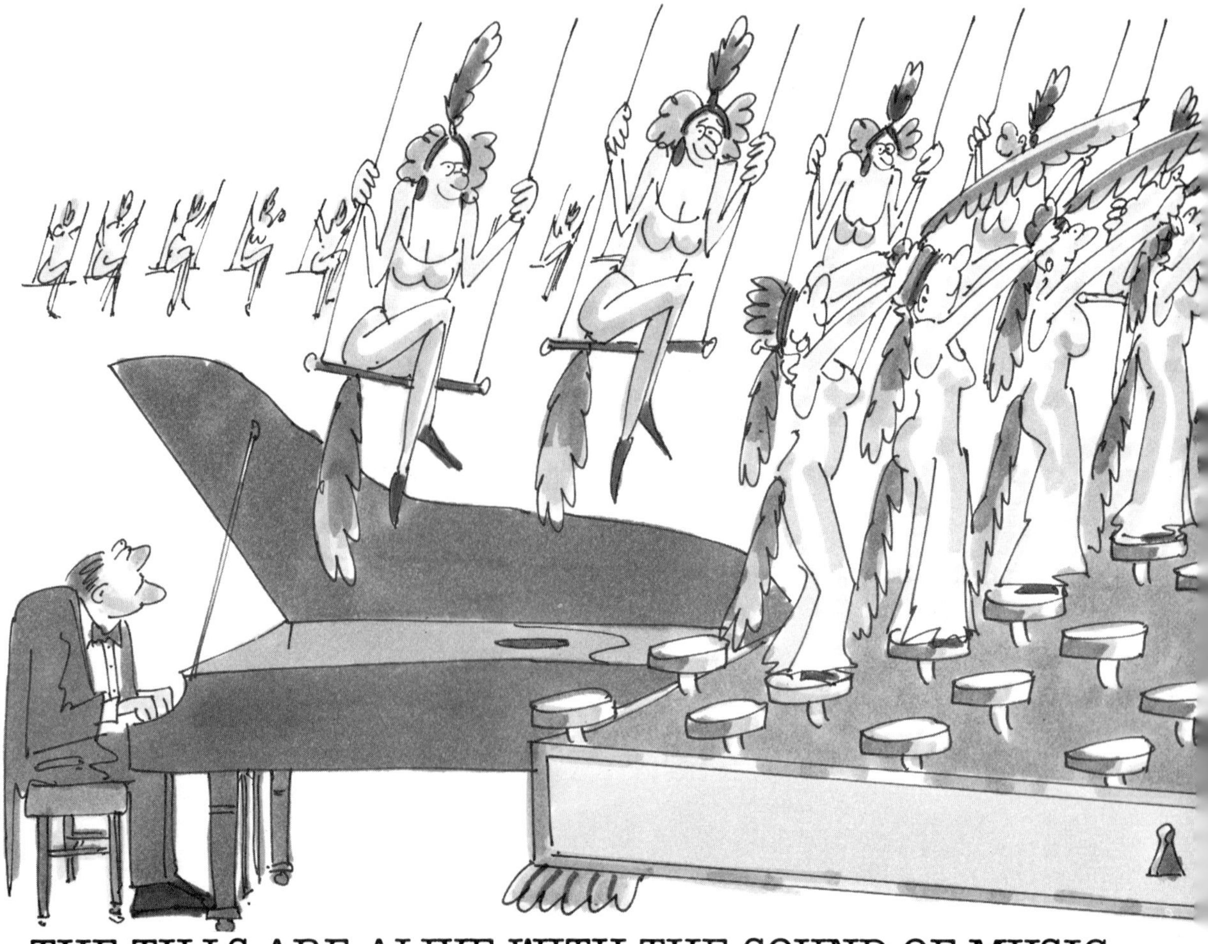

THE TILLS ARE ALIVE WITH THE SOUND OF MUSIC

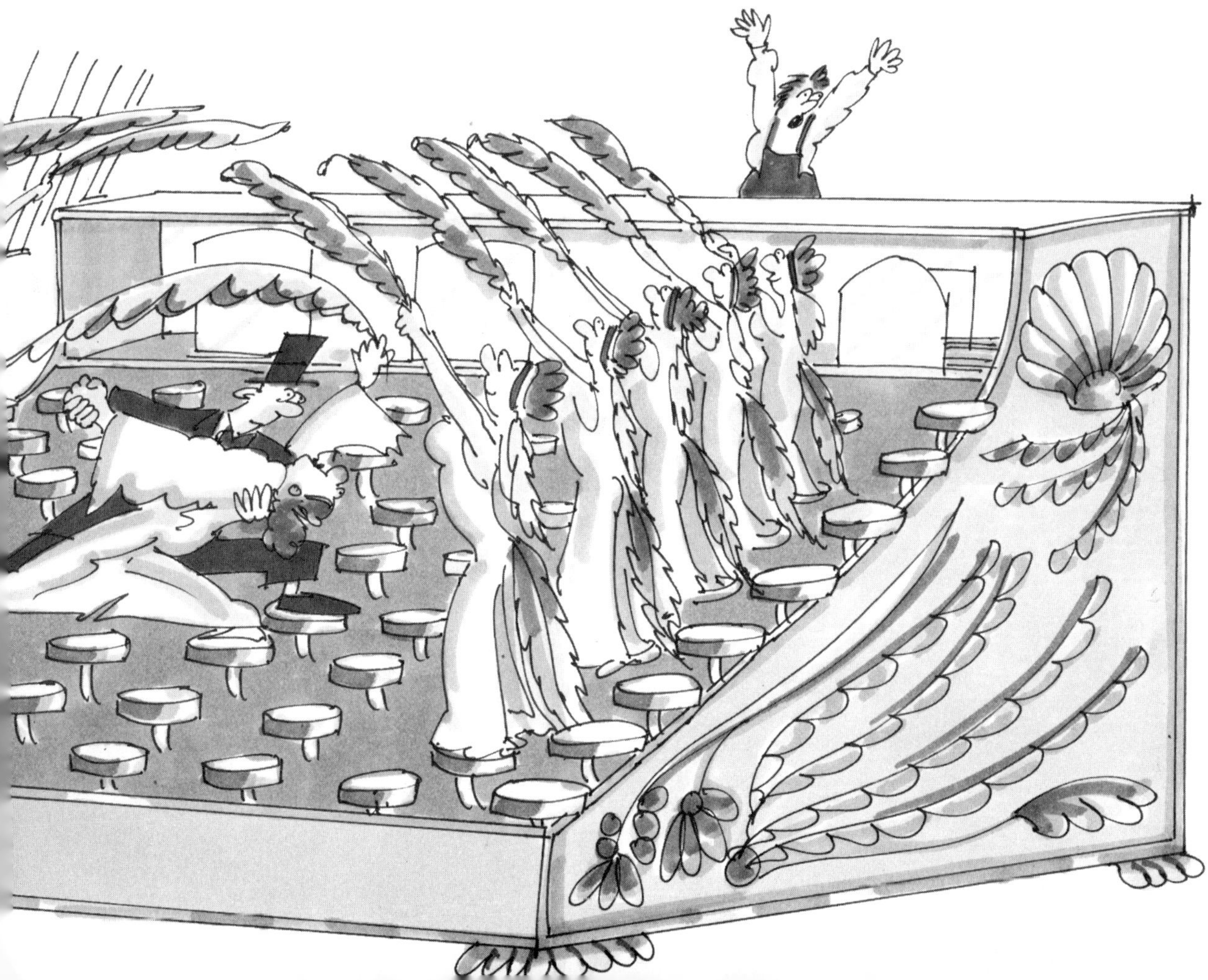

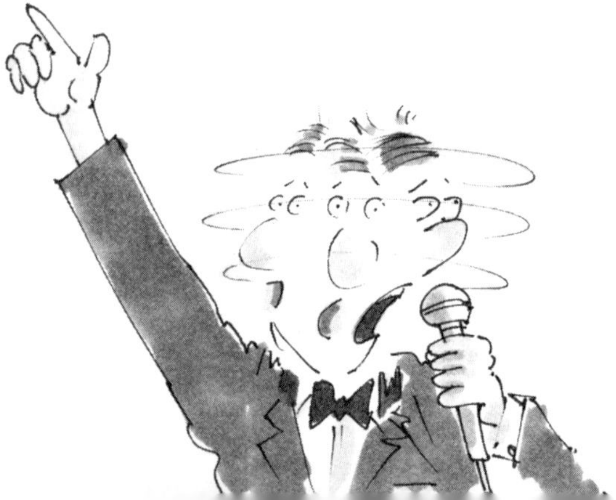

SEND IN THE CLONES

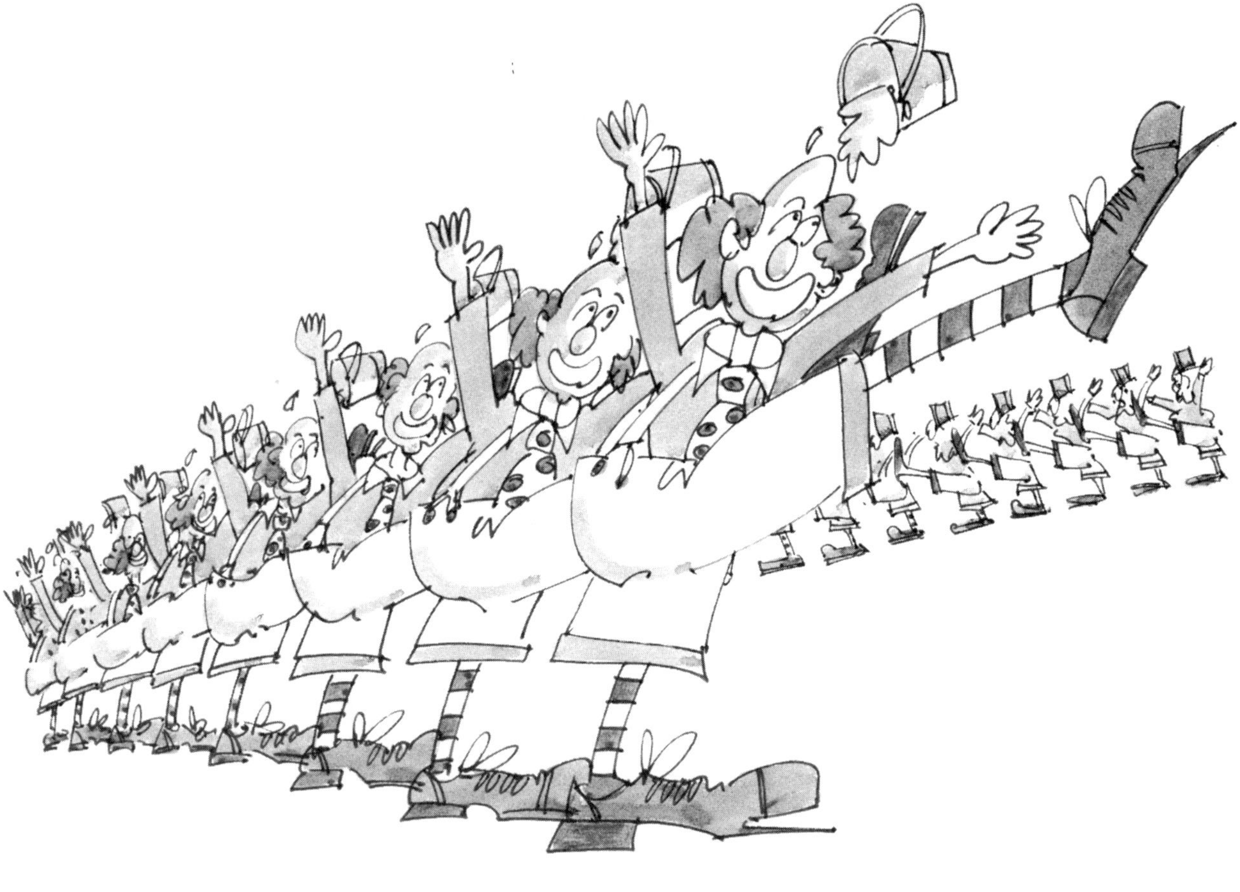

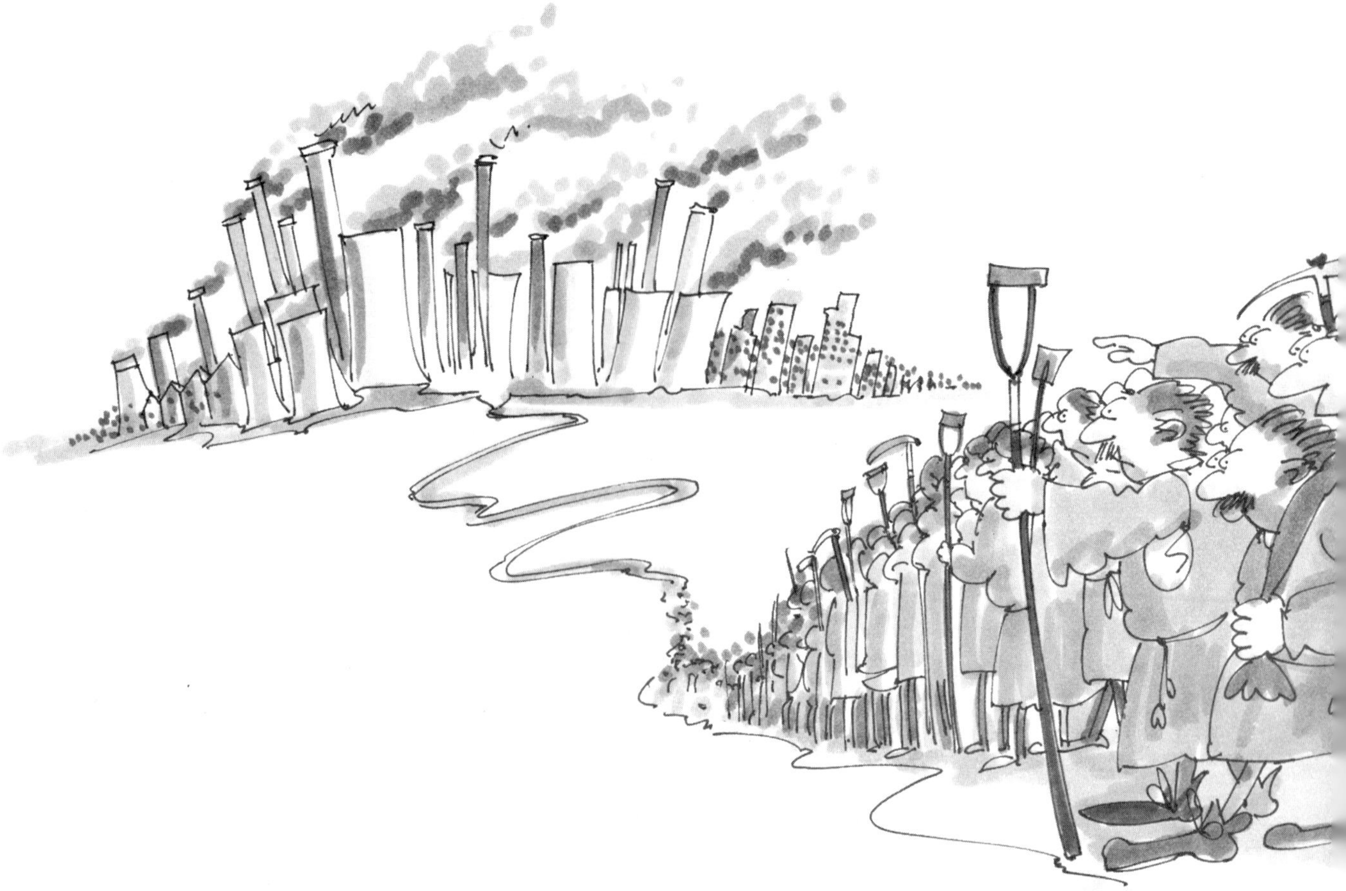

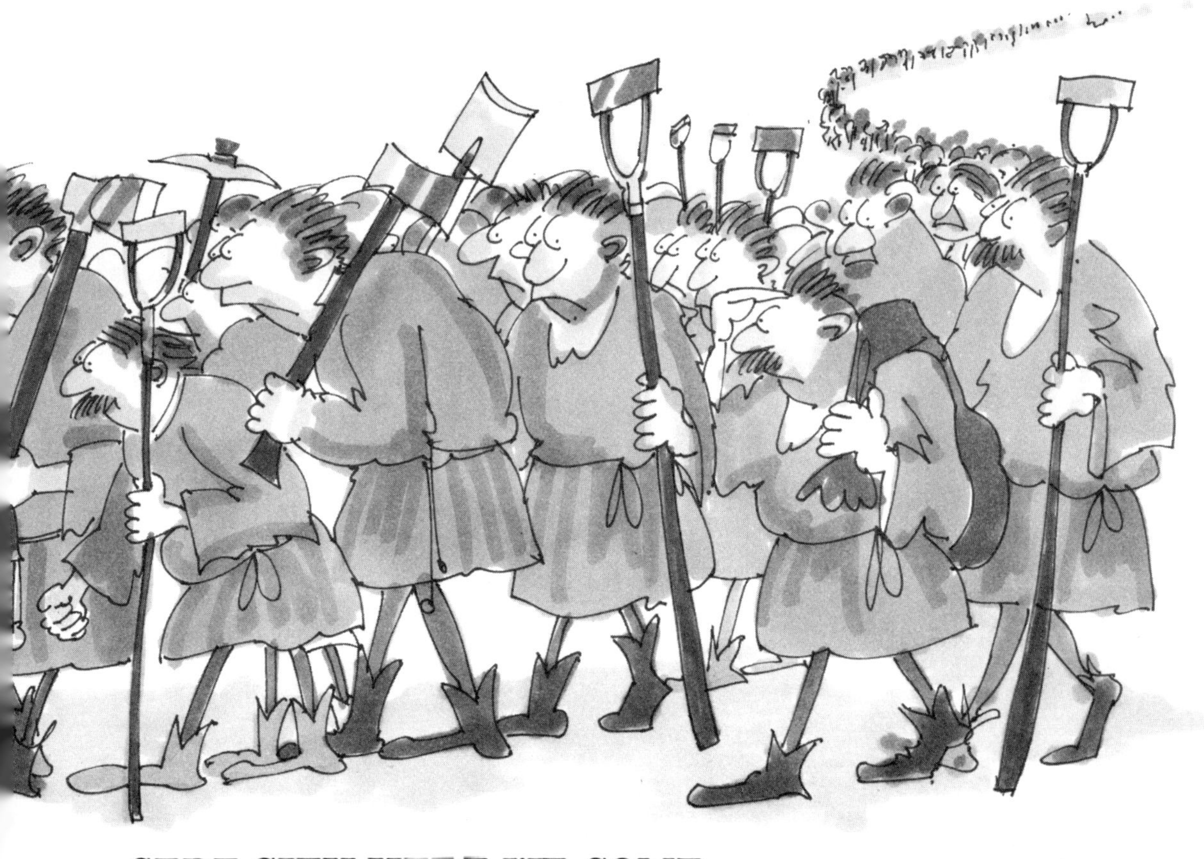

SERF CITY HERE WE COME

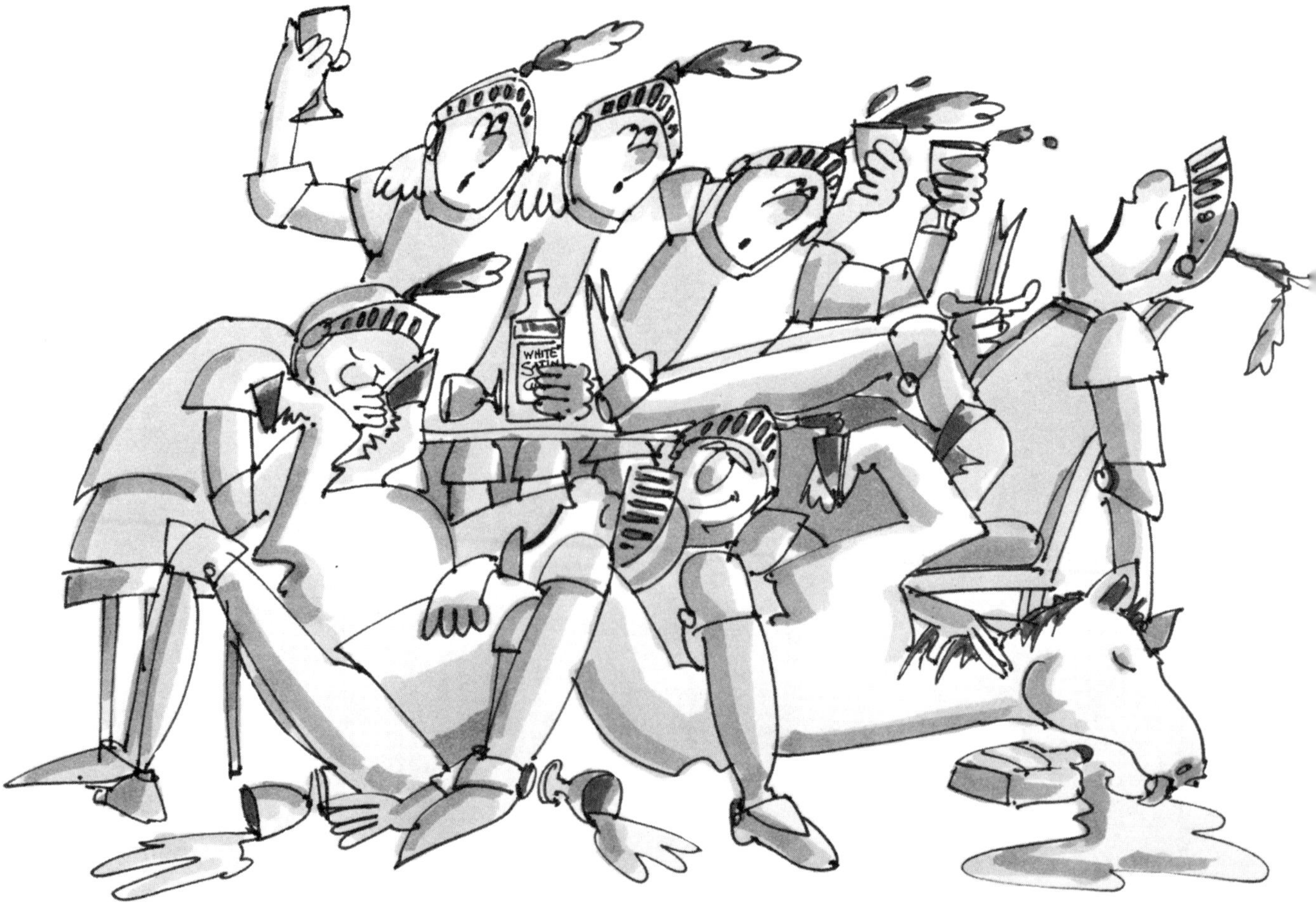
WHITE SATIN

KNIGHTS AND WHITE SATIN

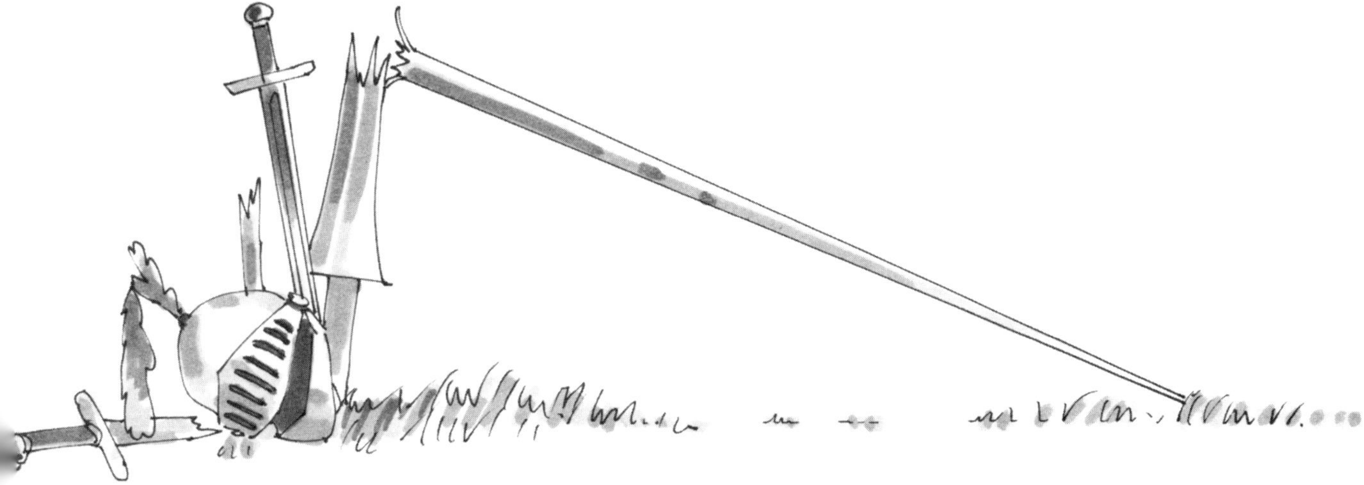

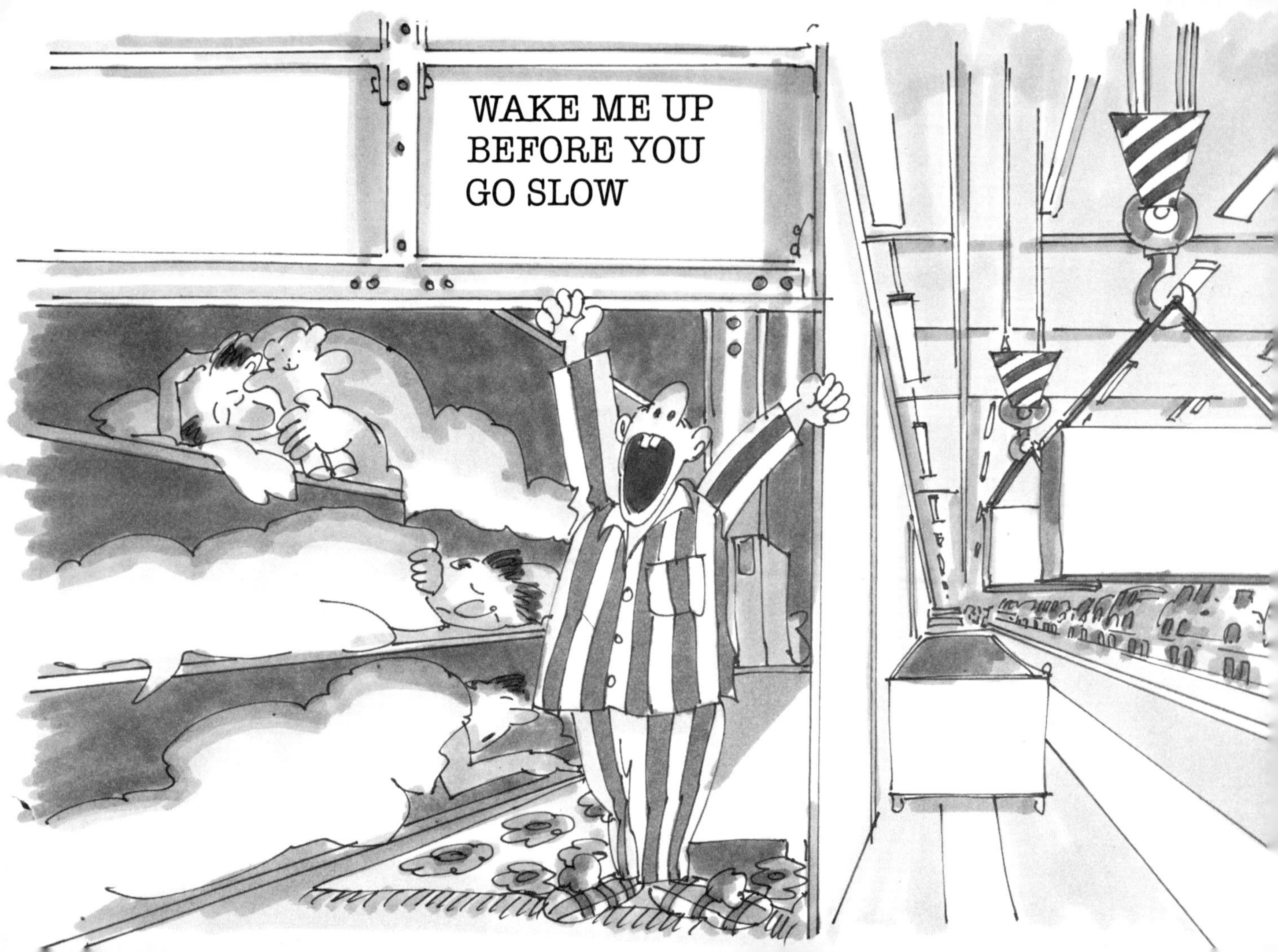
WAKE ME UP
BEFORE YOU
GO SLOW

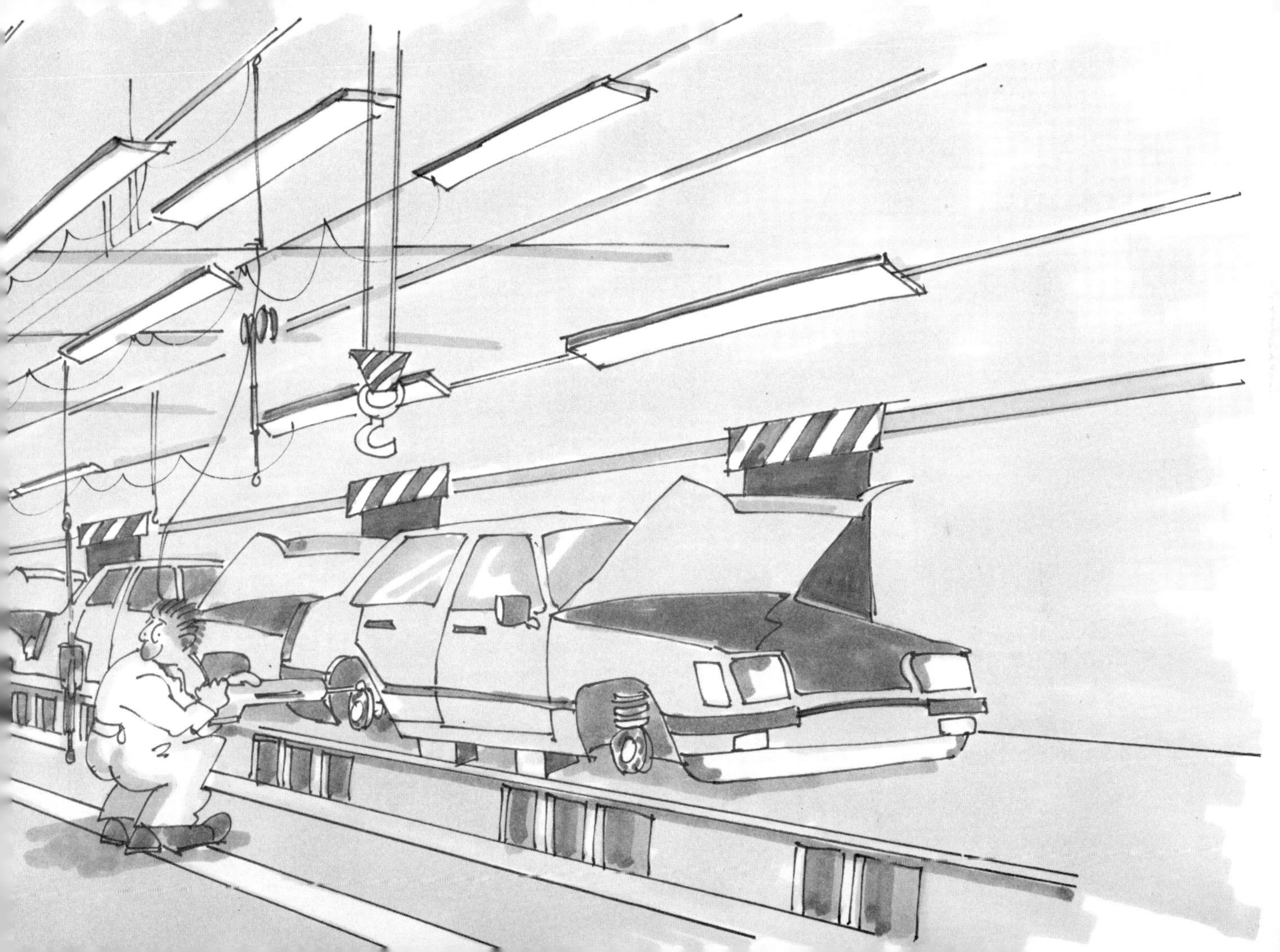

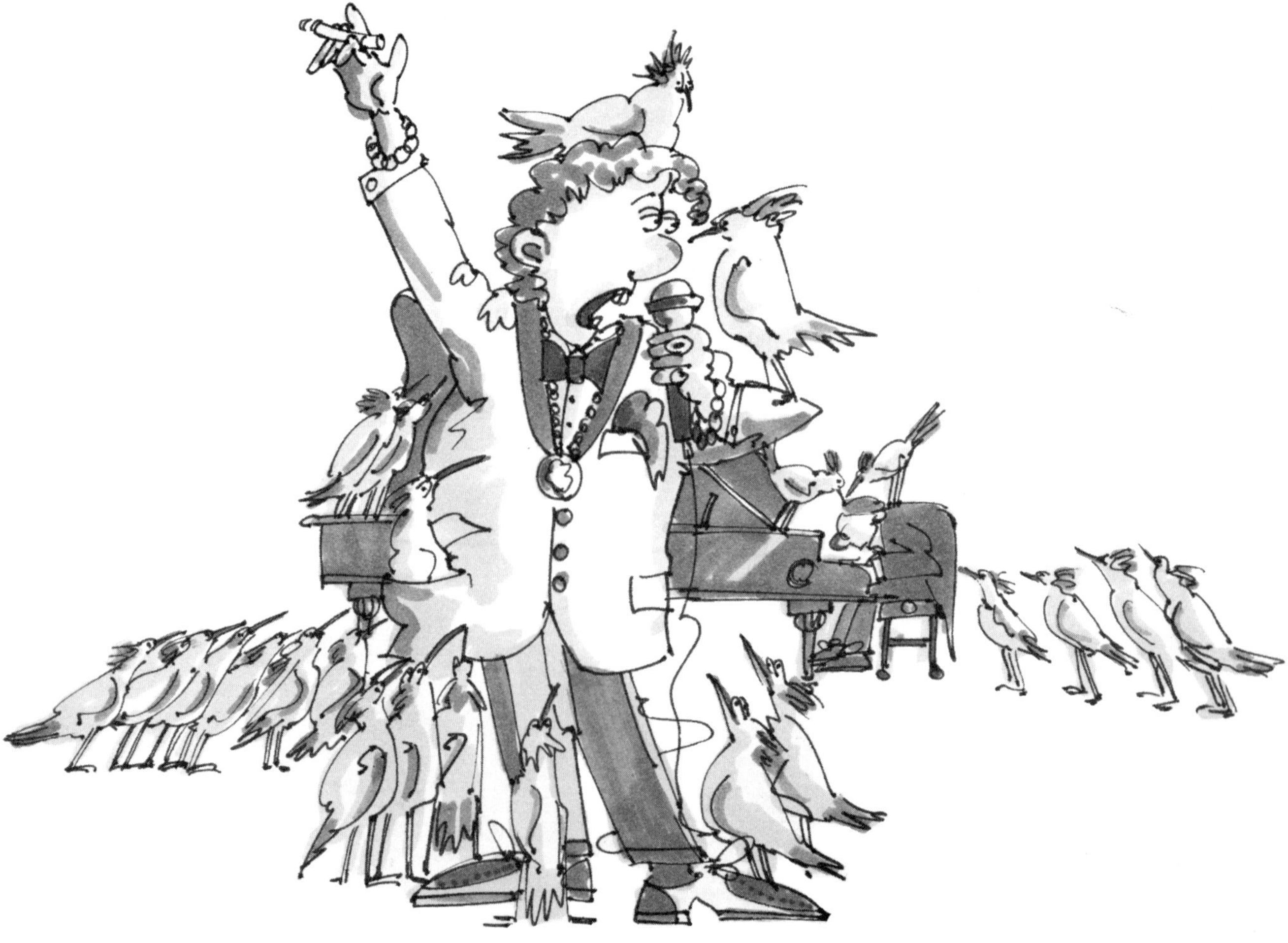

EGRETS, I'VE HAD A FEW

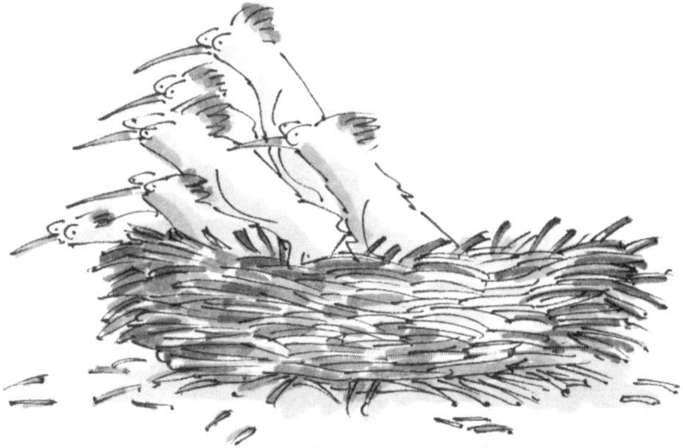

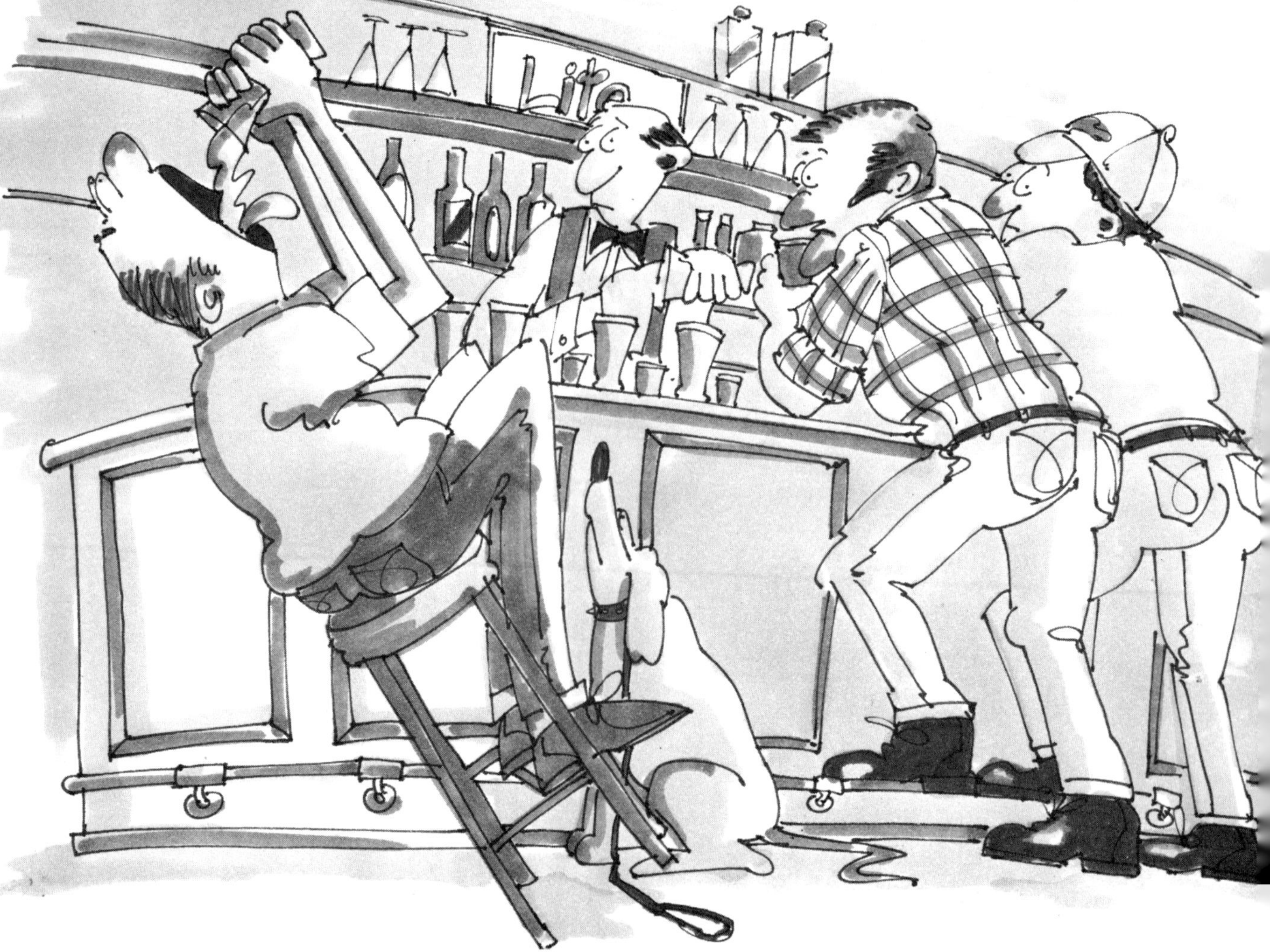

WELL I NEVER FELT MORE LIKE SWIGGING THE BOOZE

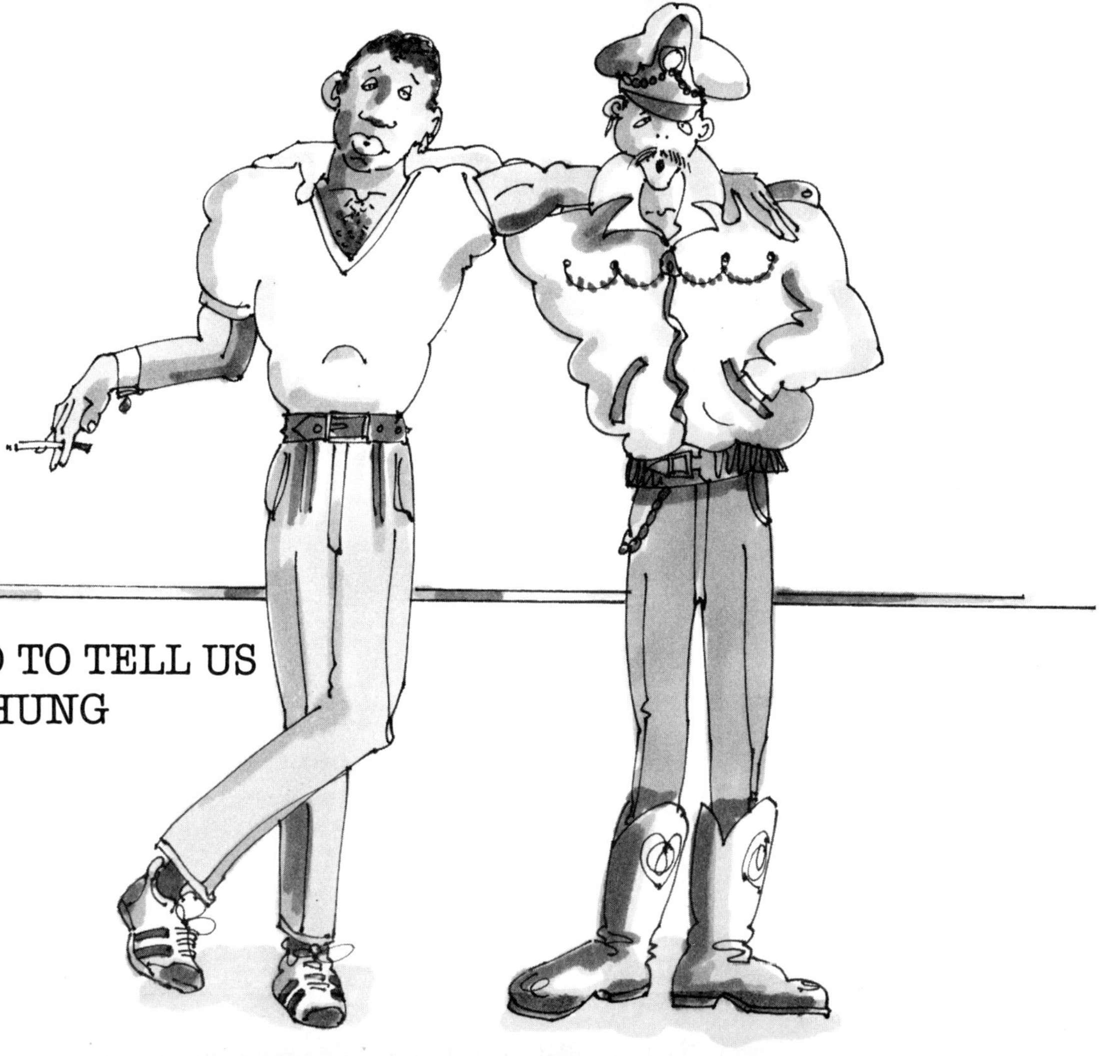

THEY TRIED TO TELL US
WE'RE TOO HUNG

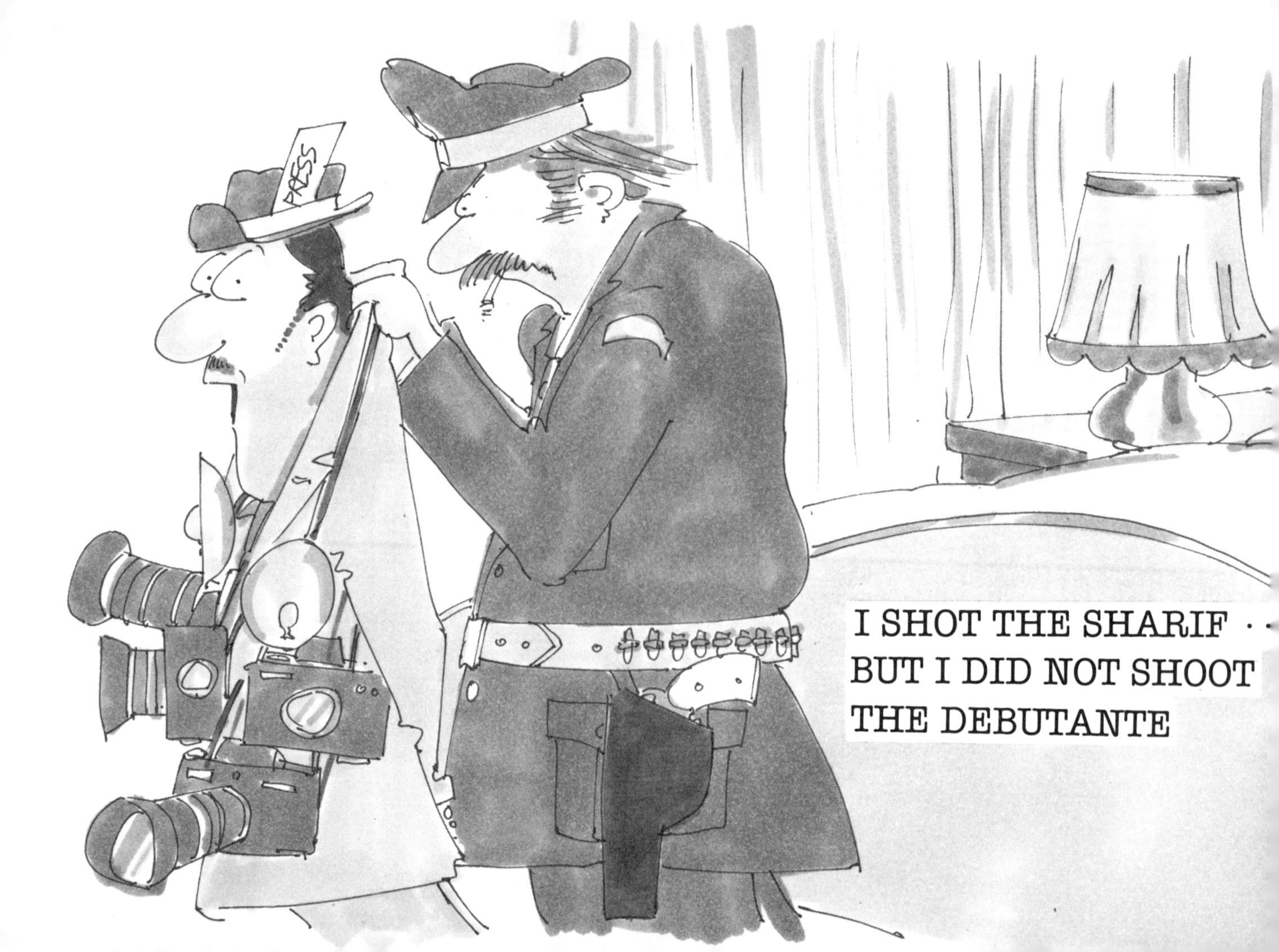

I SHOT THE SHARIF . .
BUT I DID NOT SHOOT
THE DEBUTANTE

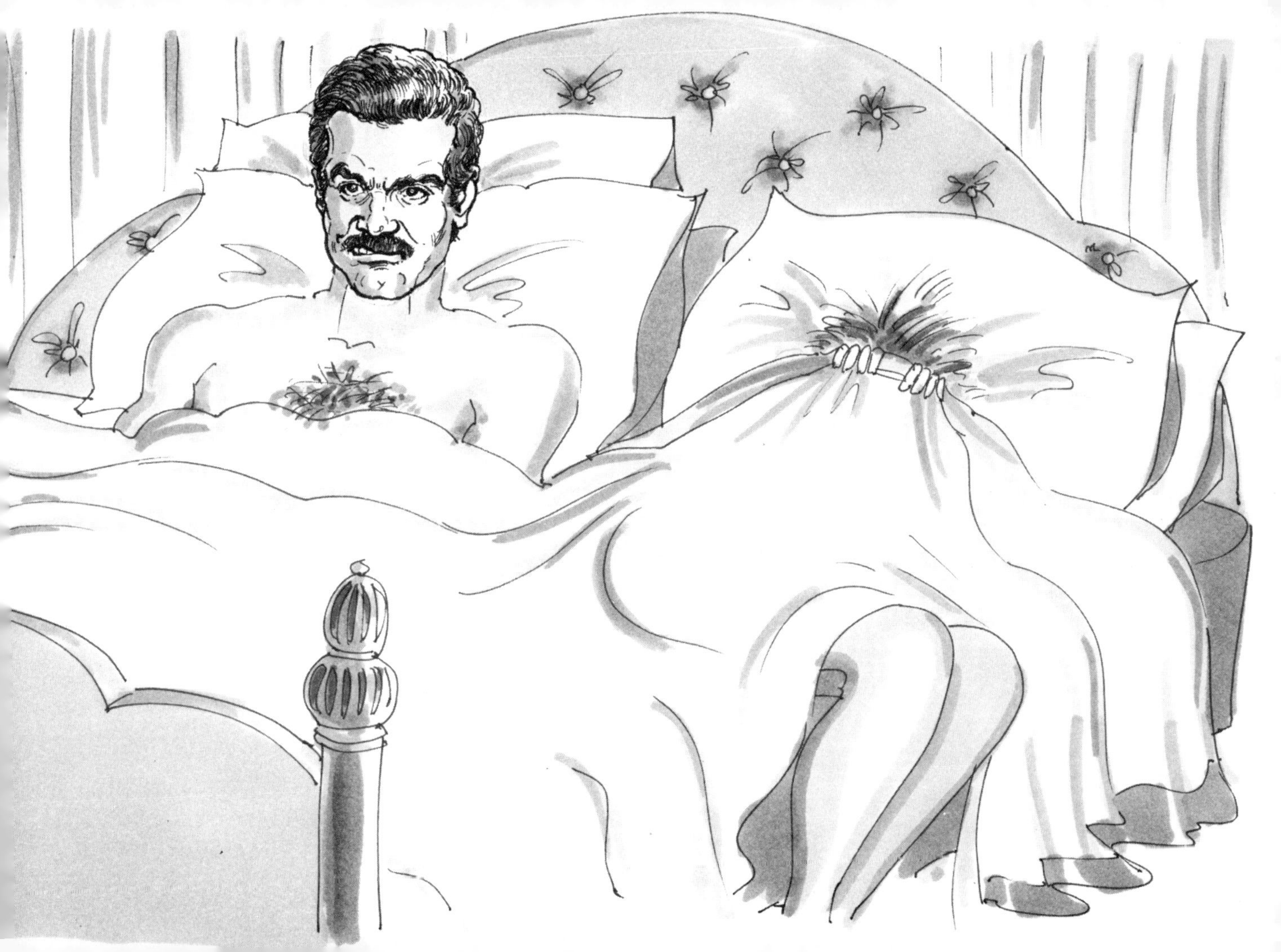

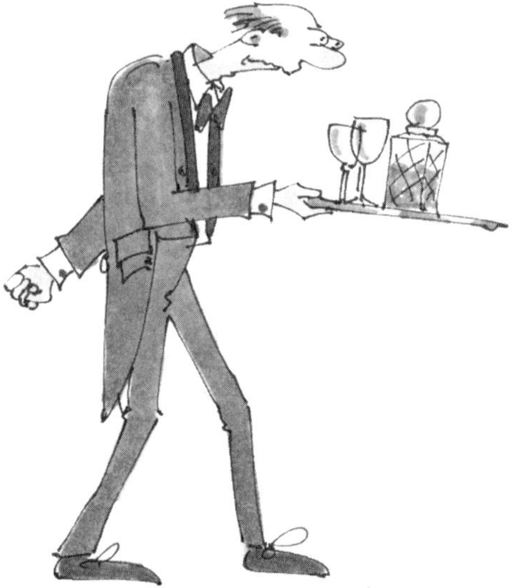

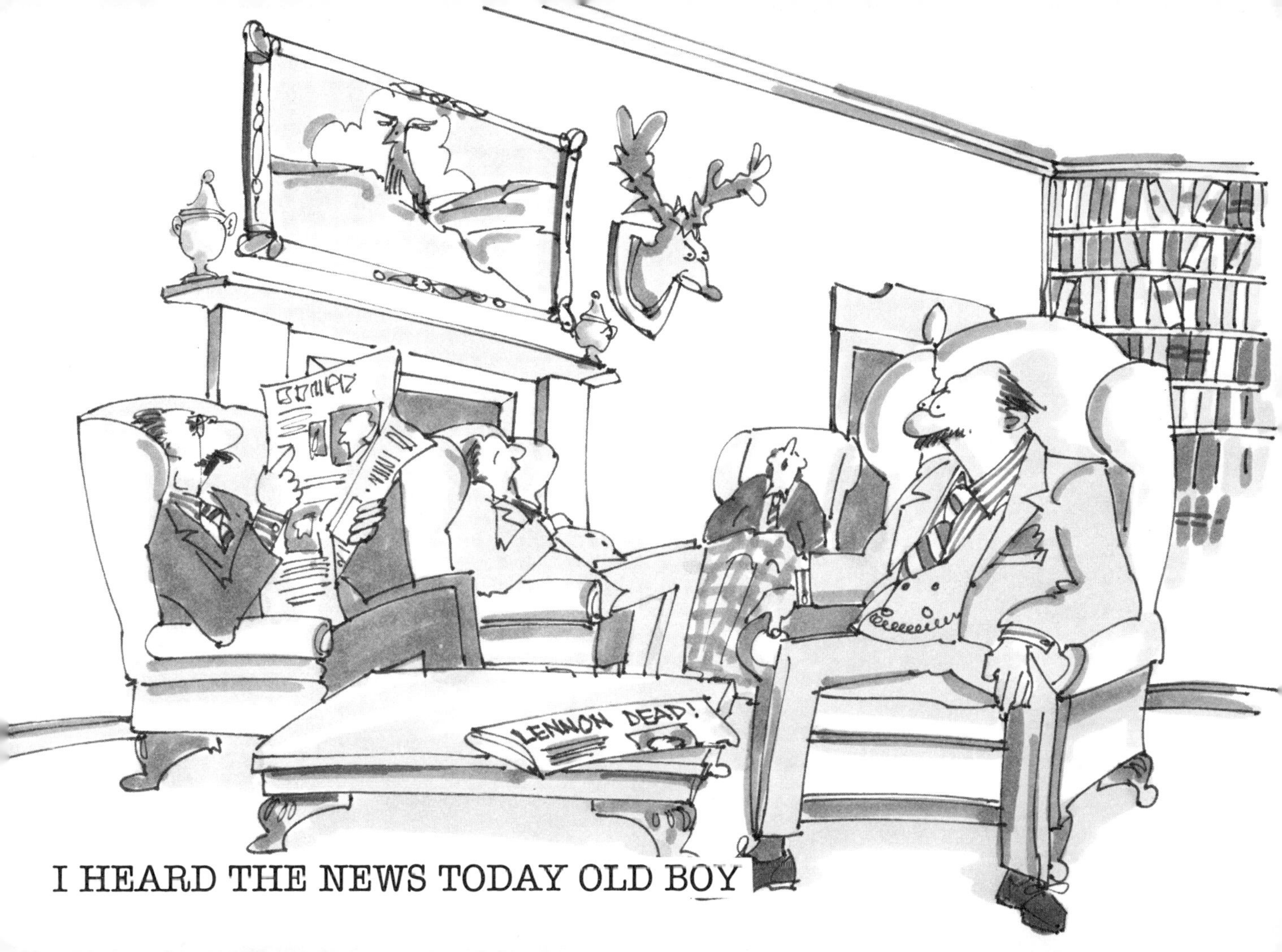

I HEARD THE NEWS TODAY OLD BOY

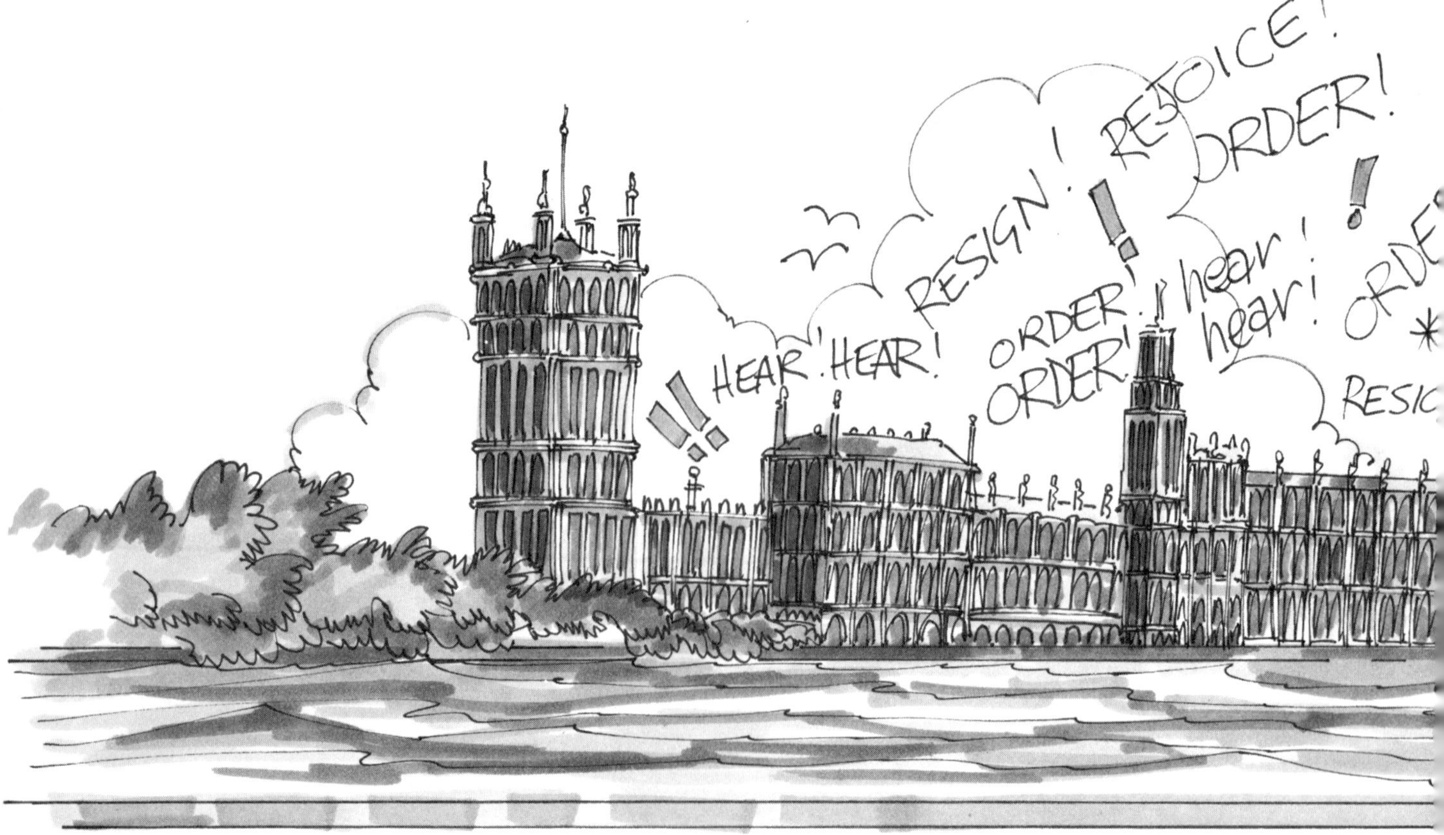
HEAR! HEAR!
RESIGN!
RESJOICE!
ORDER!
ORDER!
ORDER!
hear! hear!

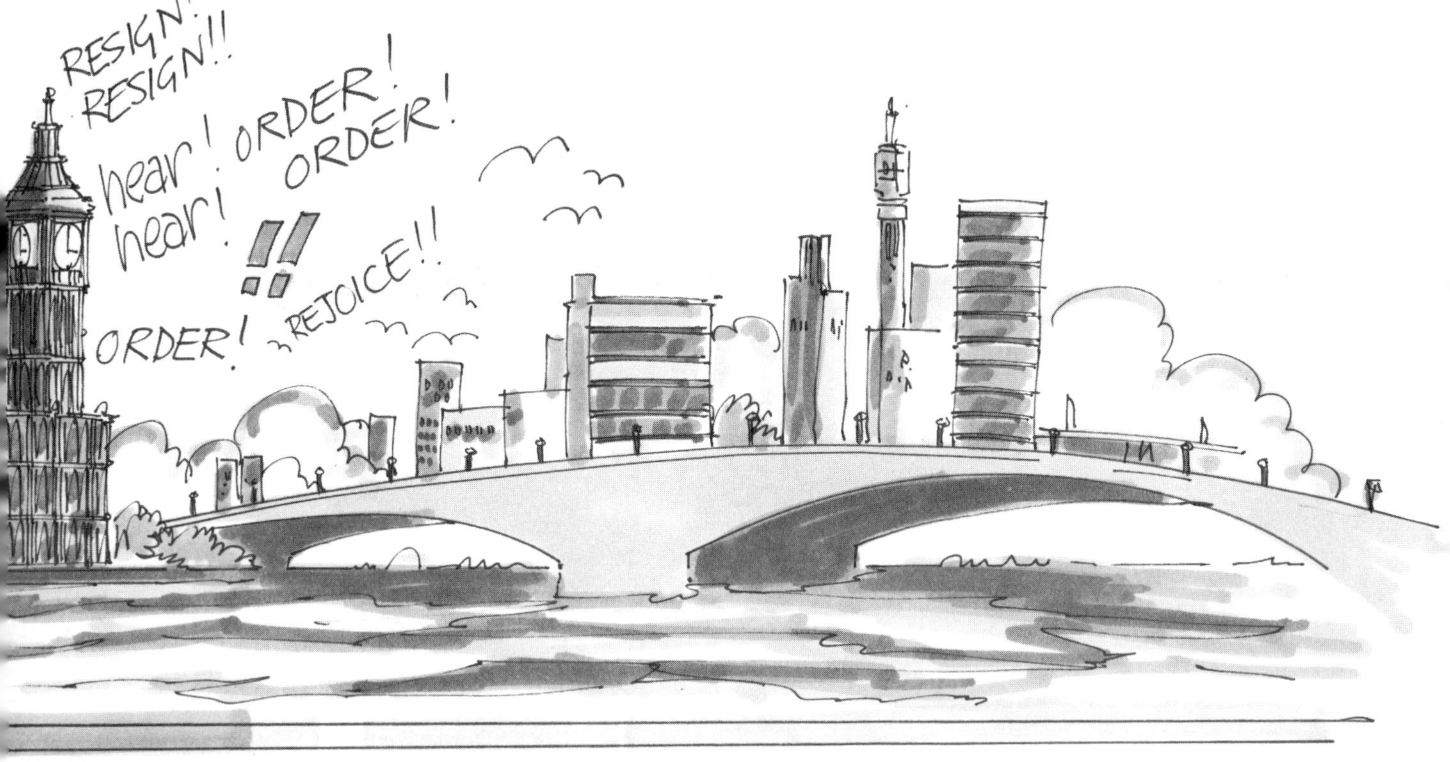

BY THE RIVERS OF BABBLE ON

THERE'S A KIND OF LUSH ALL OVER THE WORLD

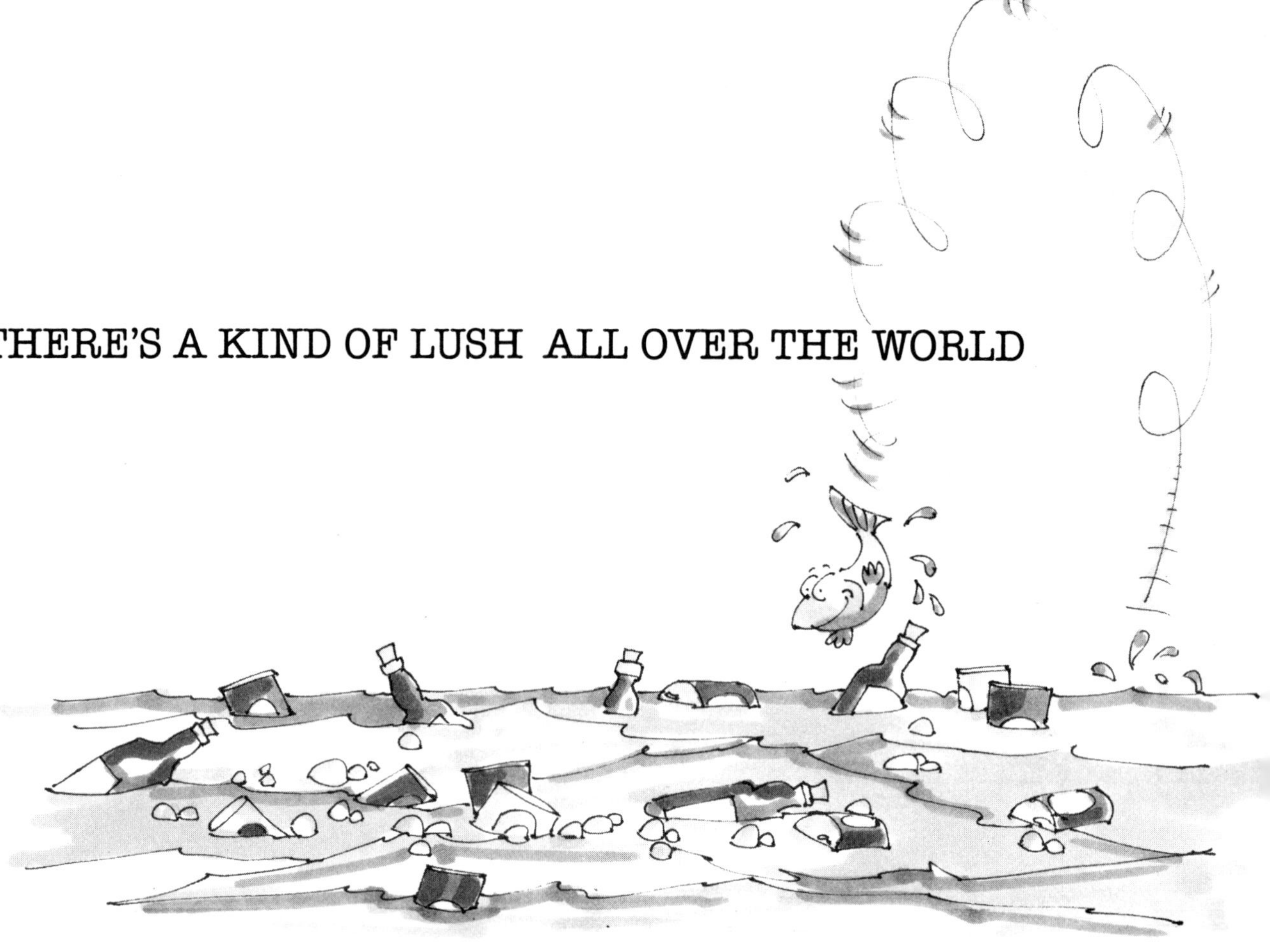

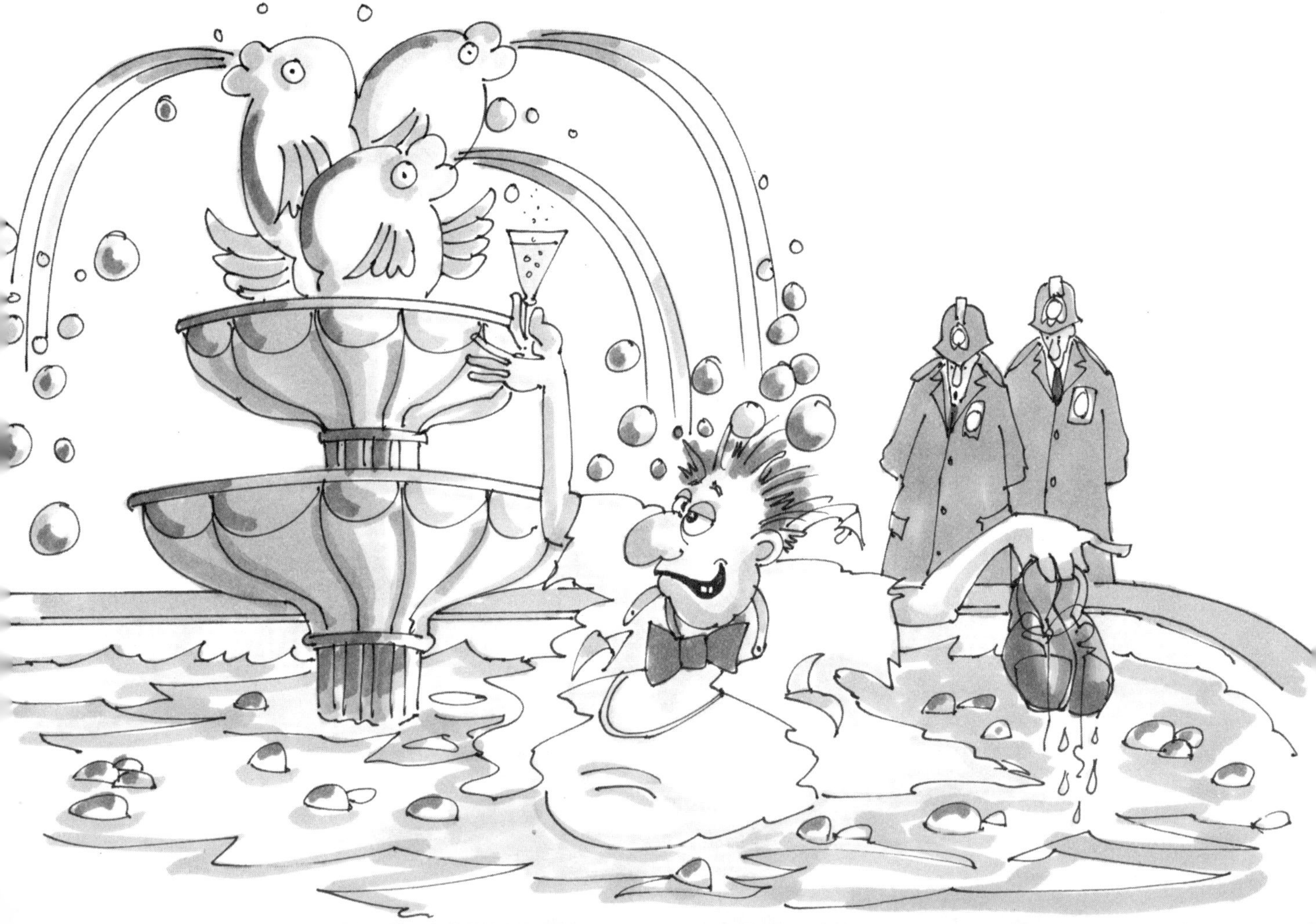

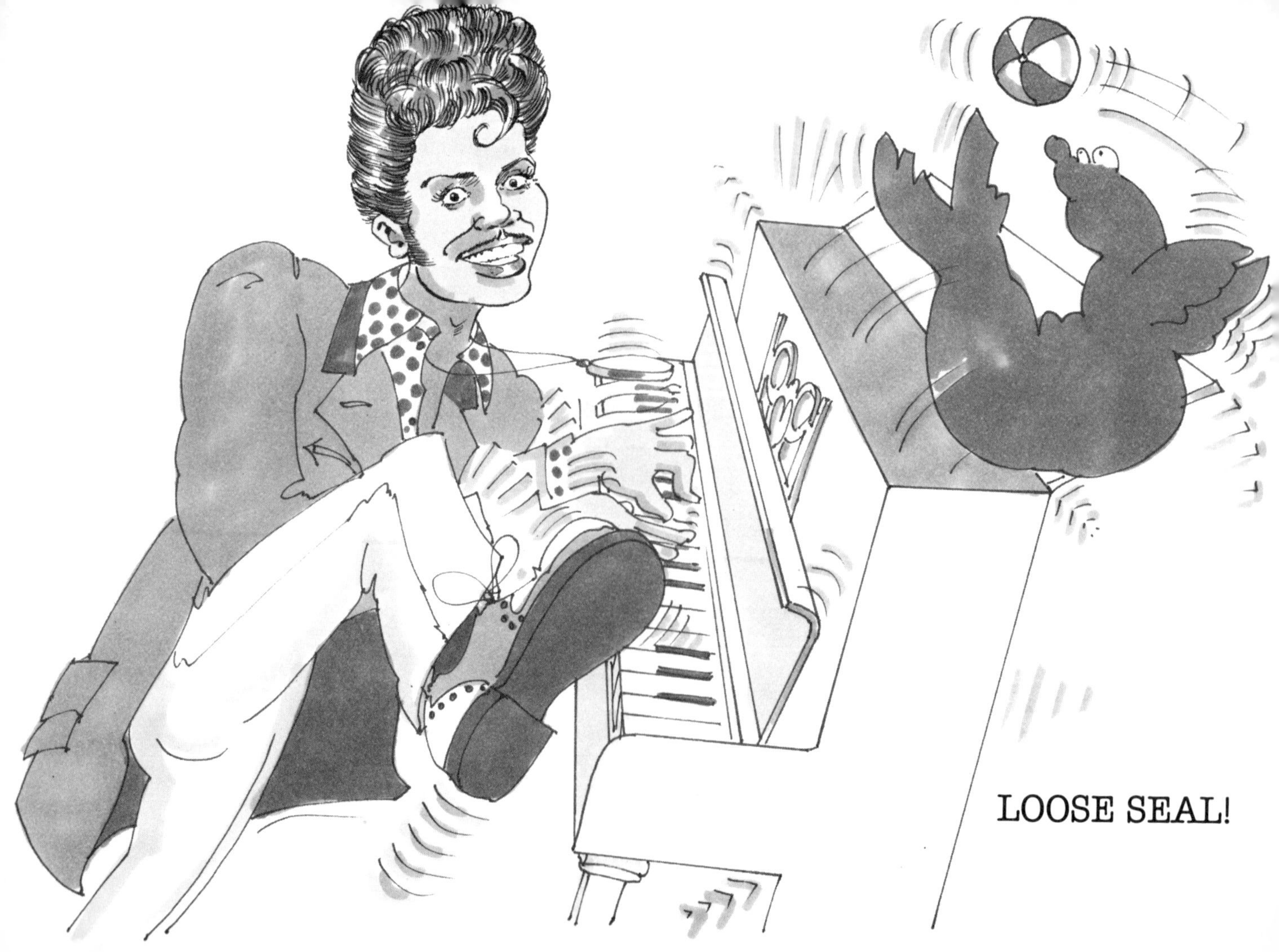

LOOSE SEAL!

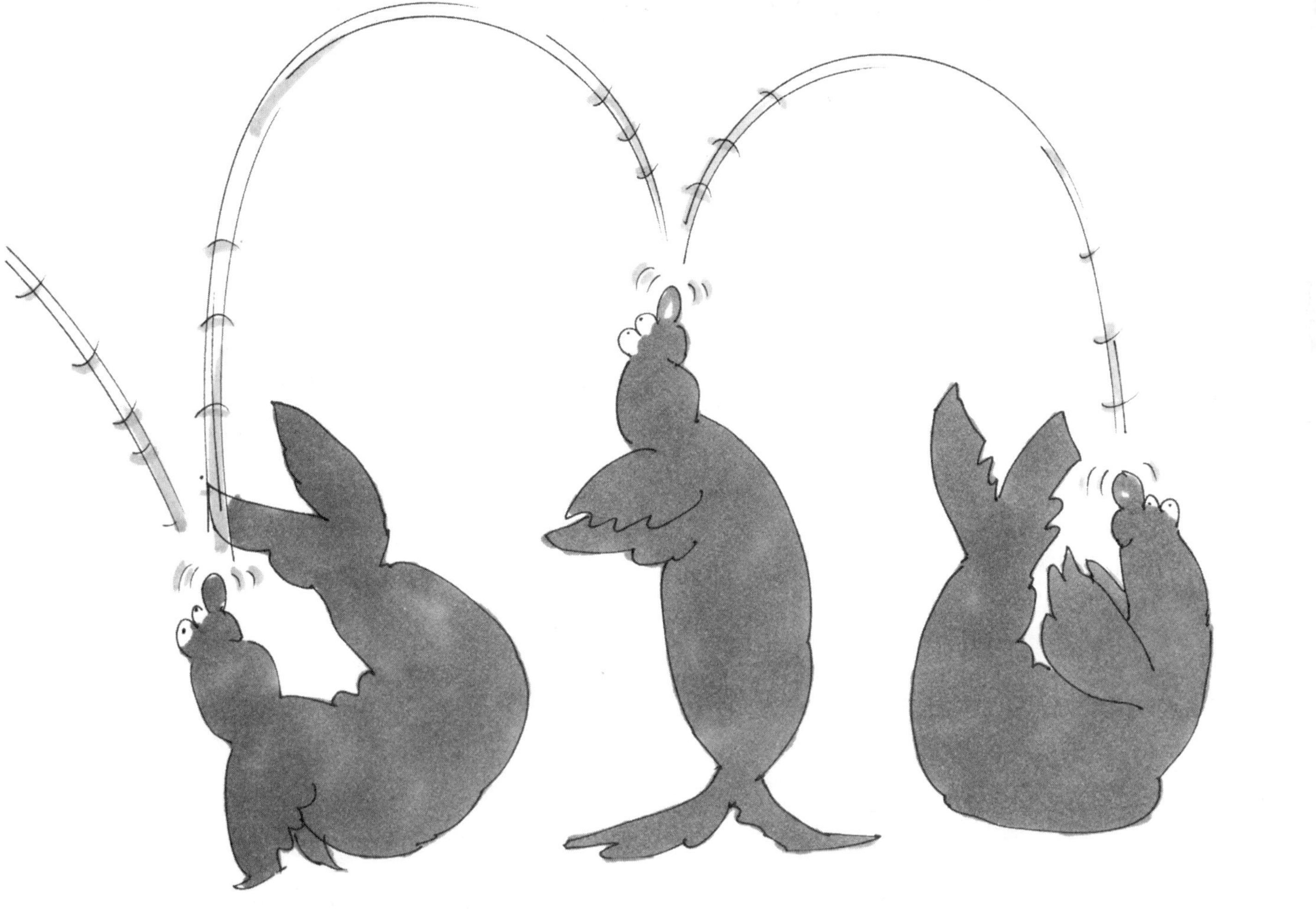

THEY'RE LOOKIN' SWELL DOLLY

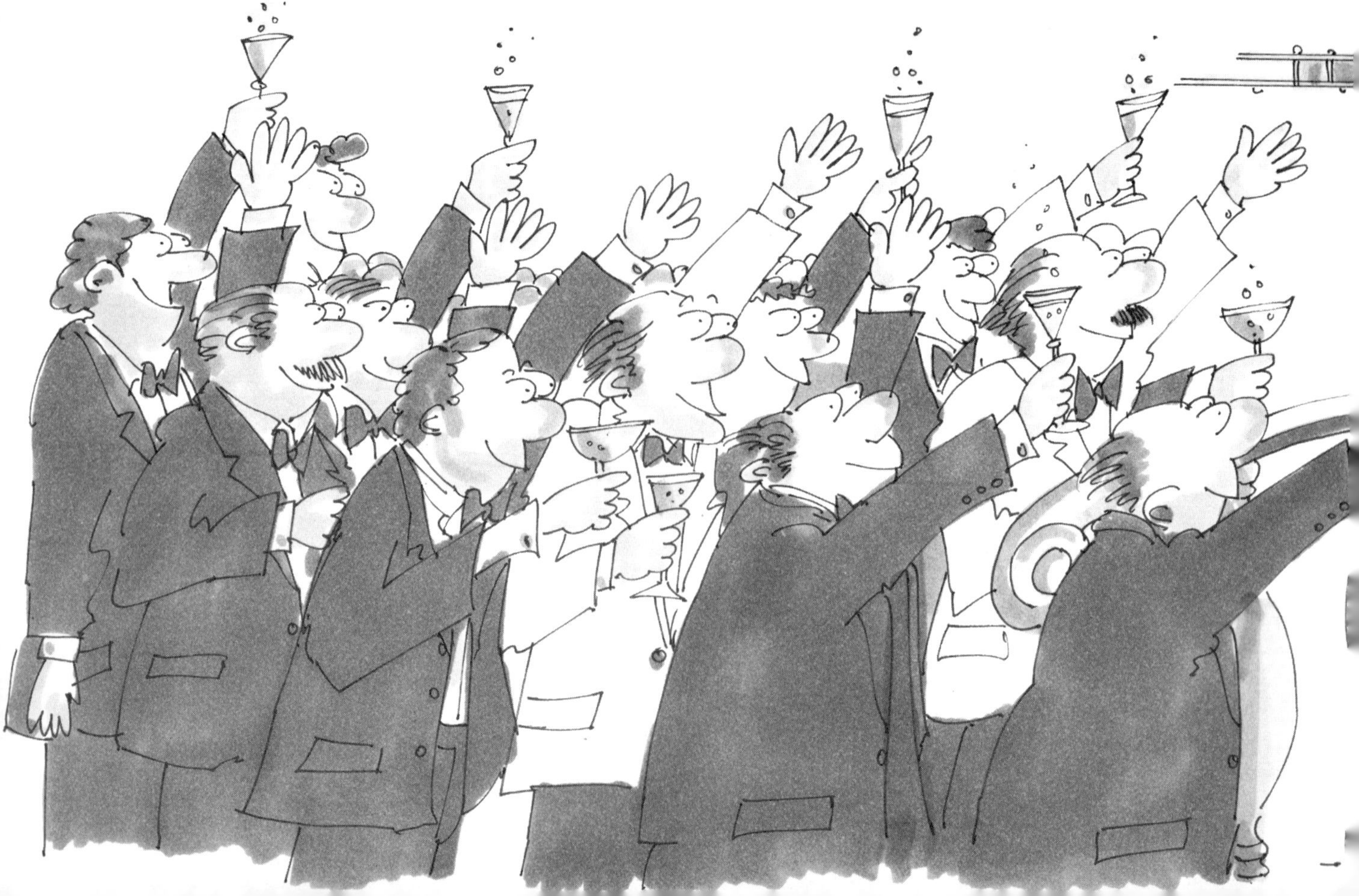

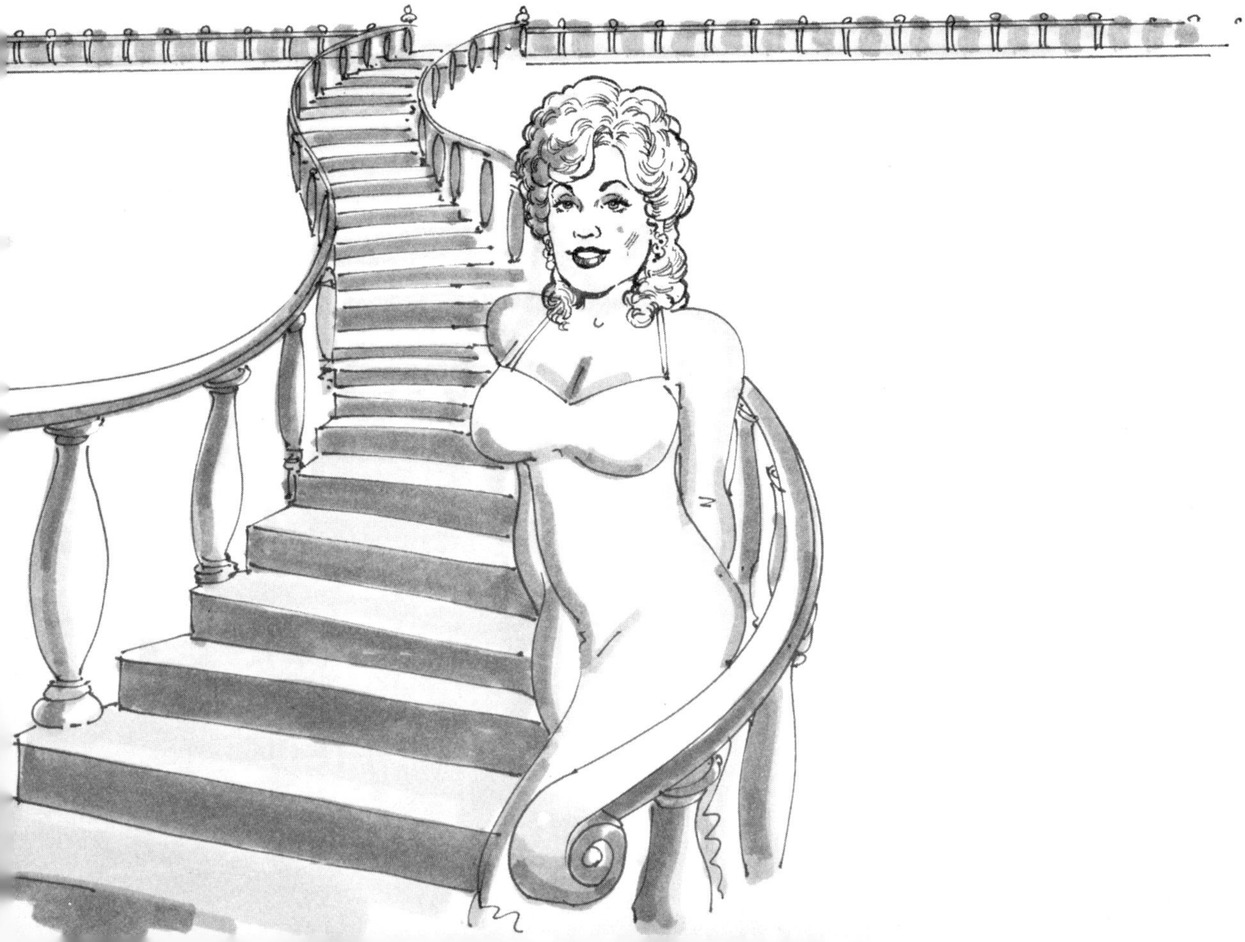

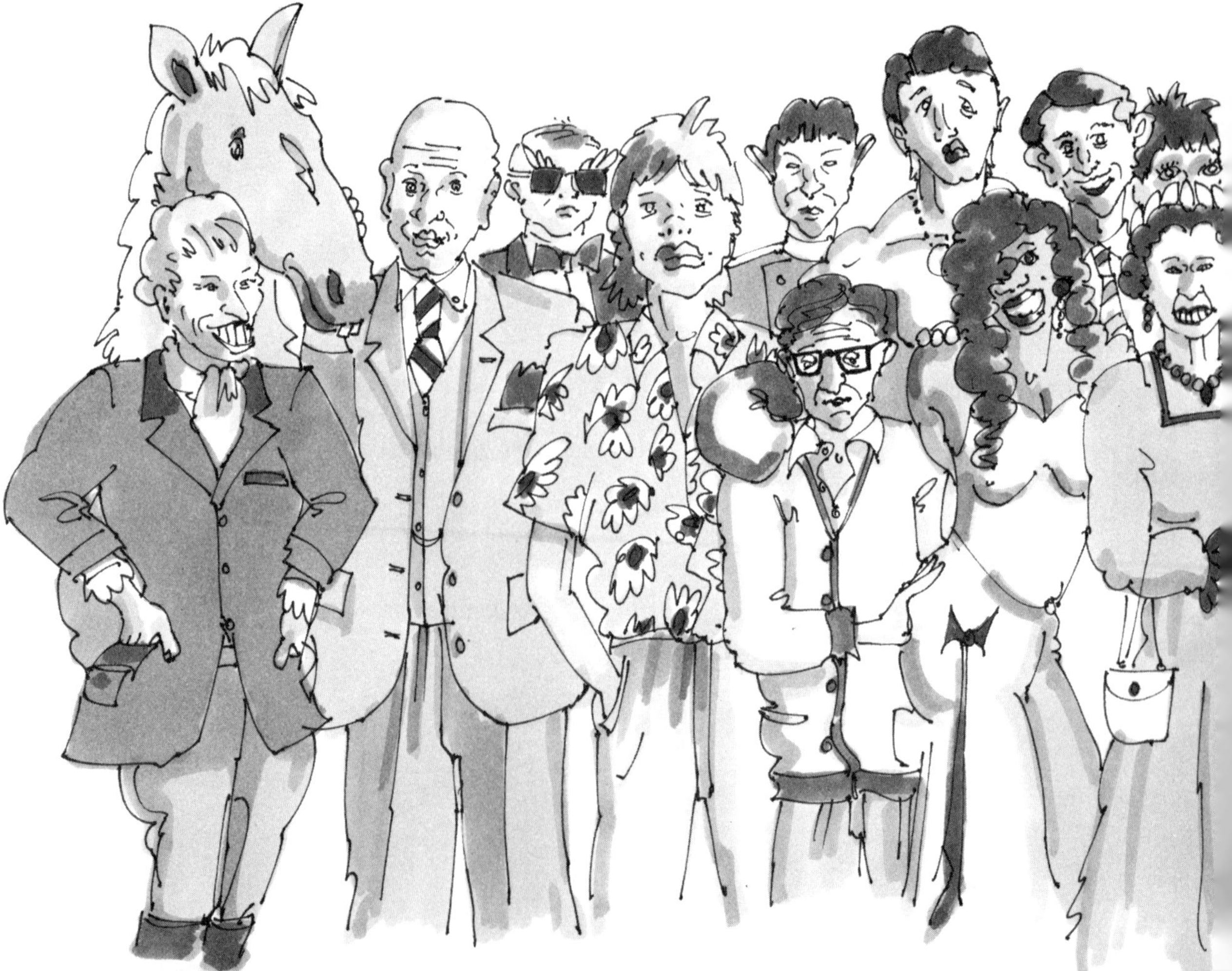

AMIN WITH THE IN CROWD

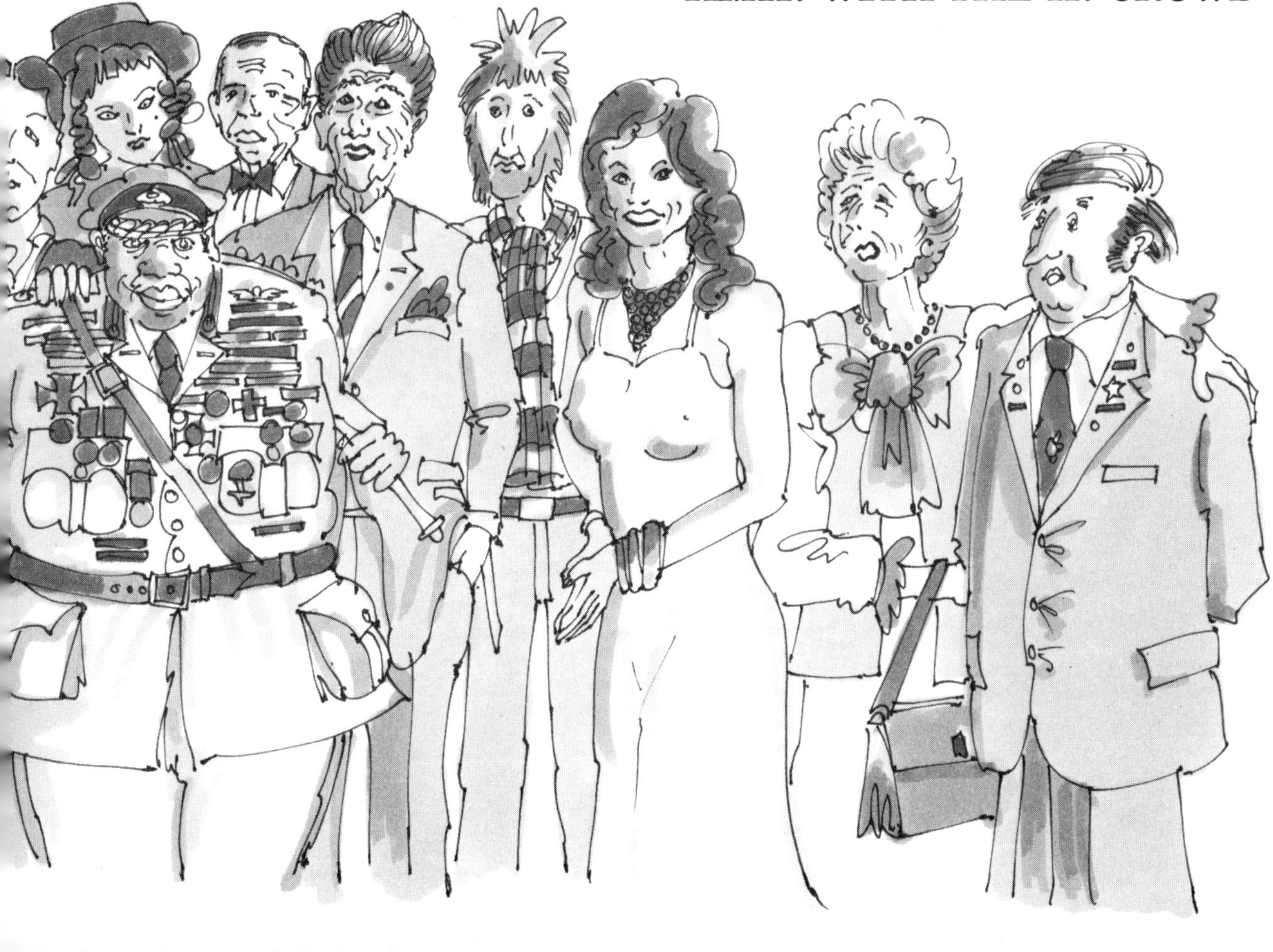

VERBS . . . VERBS DON'T COME EASY TO ME

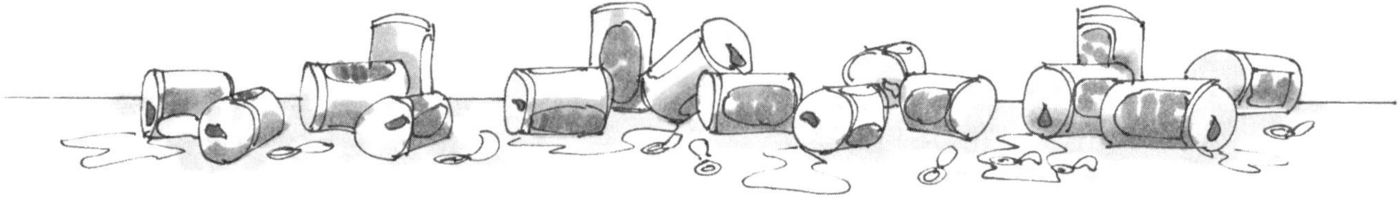

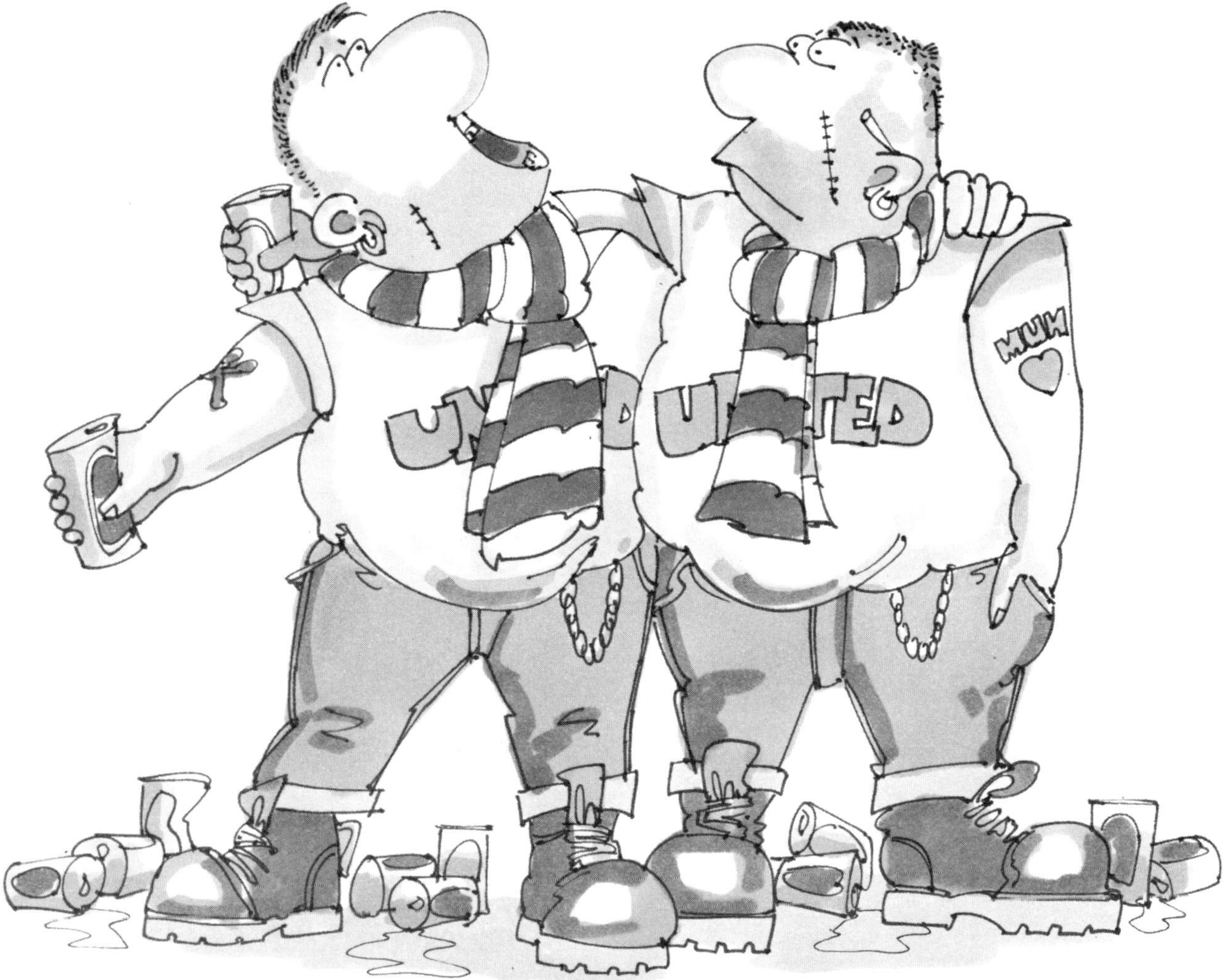
MUM

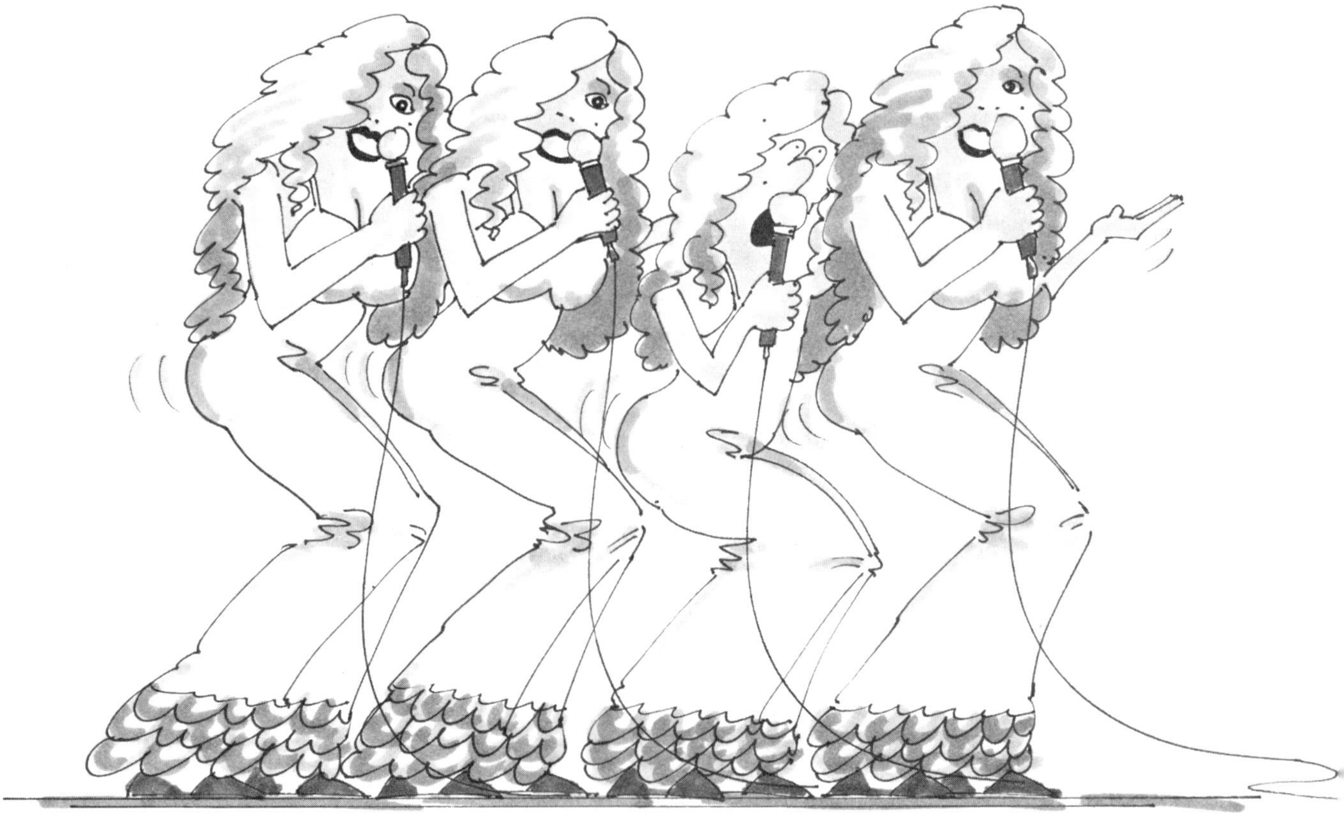

NOTHING YOU CAN SAY CAN TAKE ME AWAY FROM

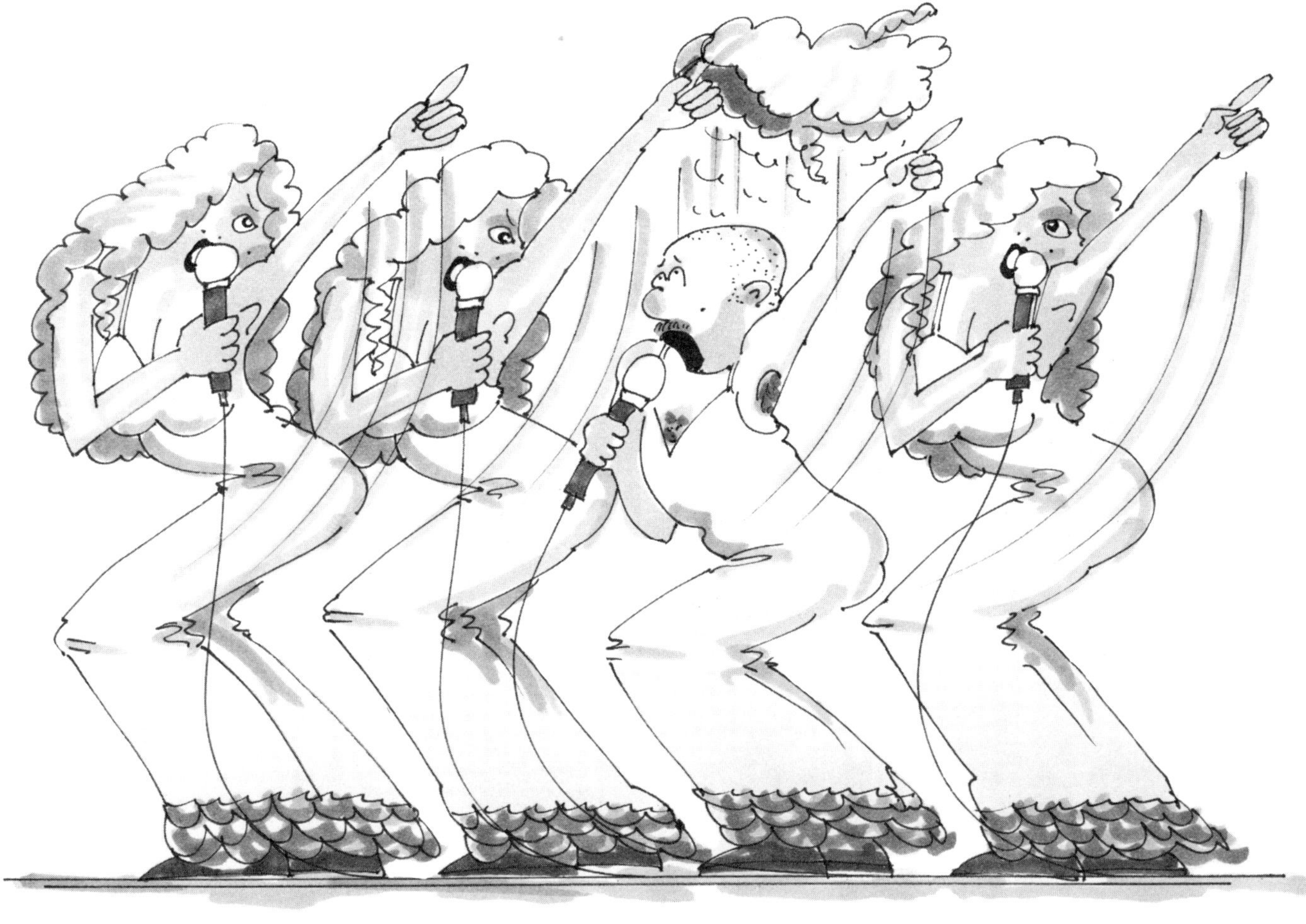

BI-GUY

WOCKY MOUNTAIN HIGH

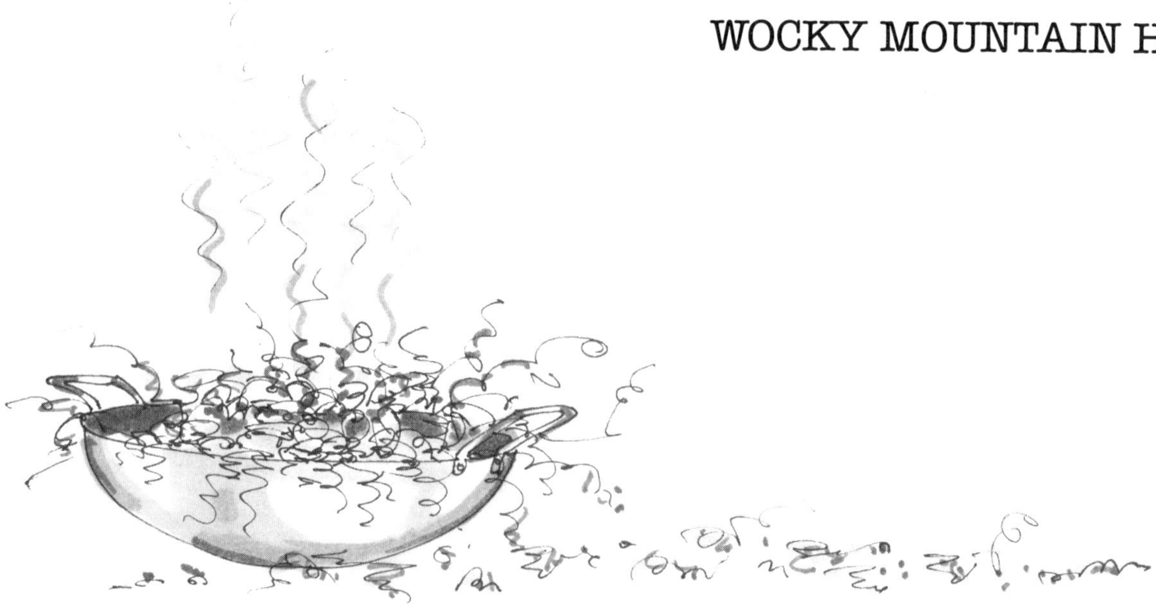

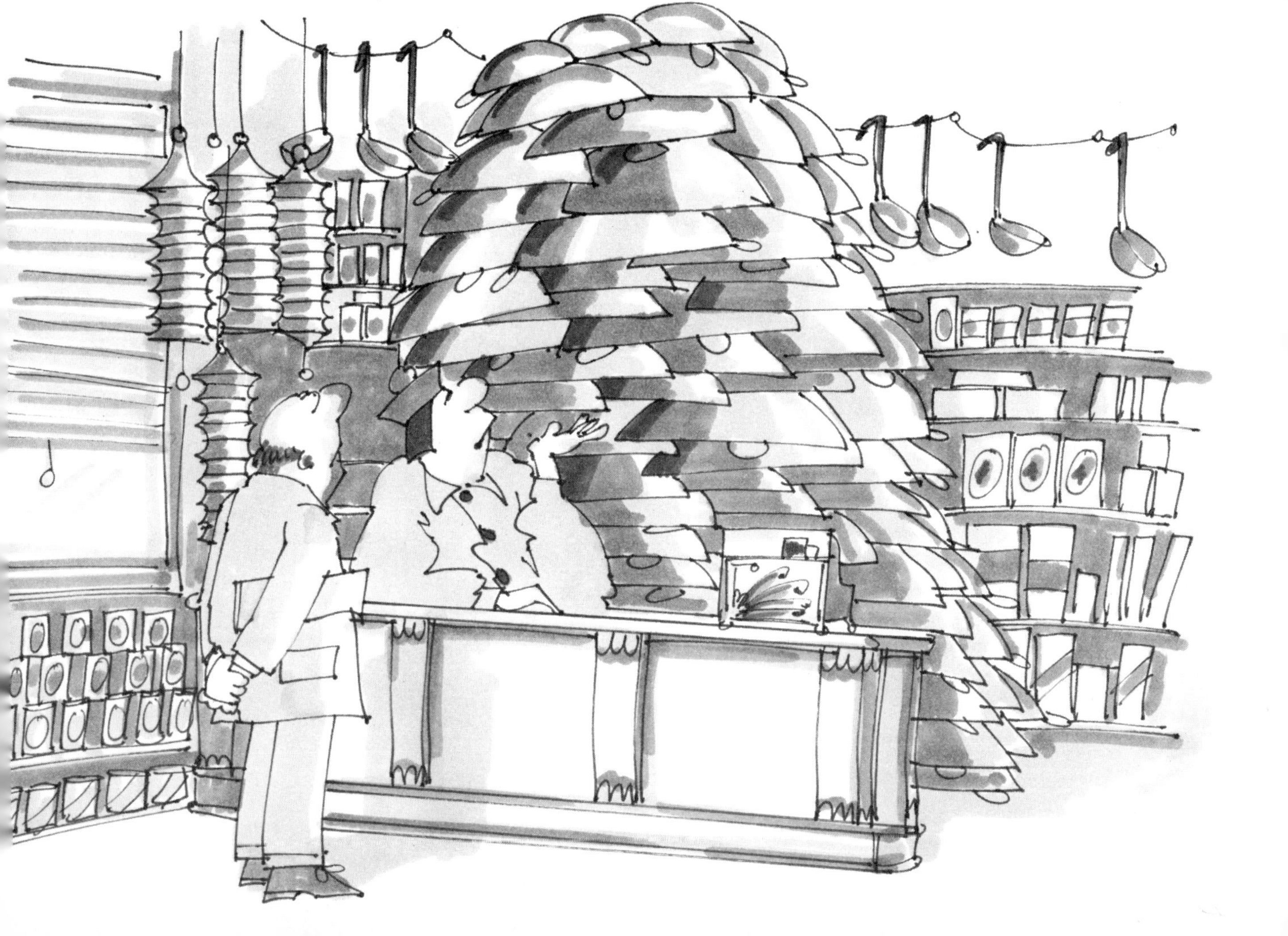

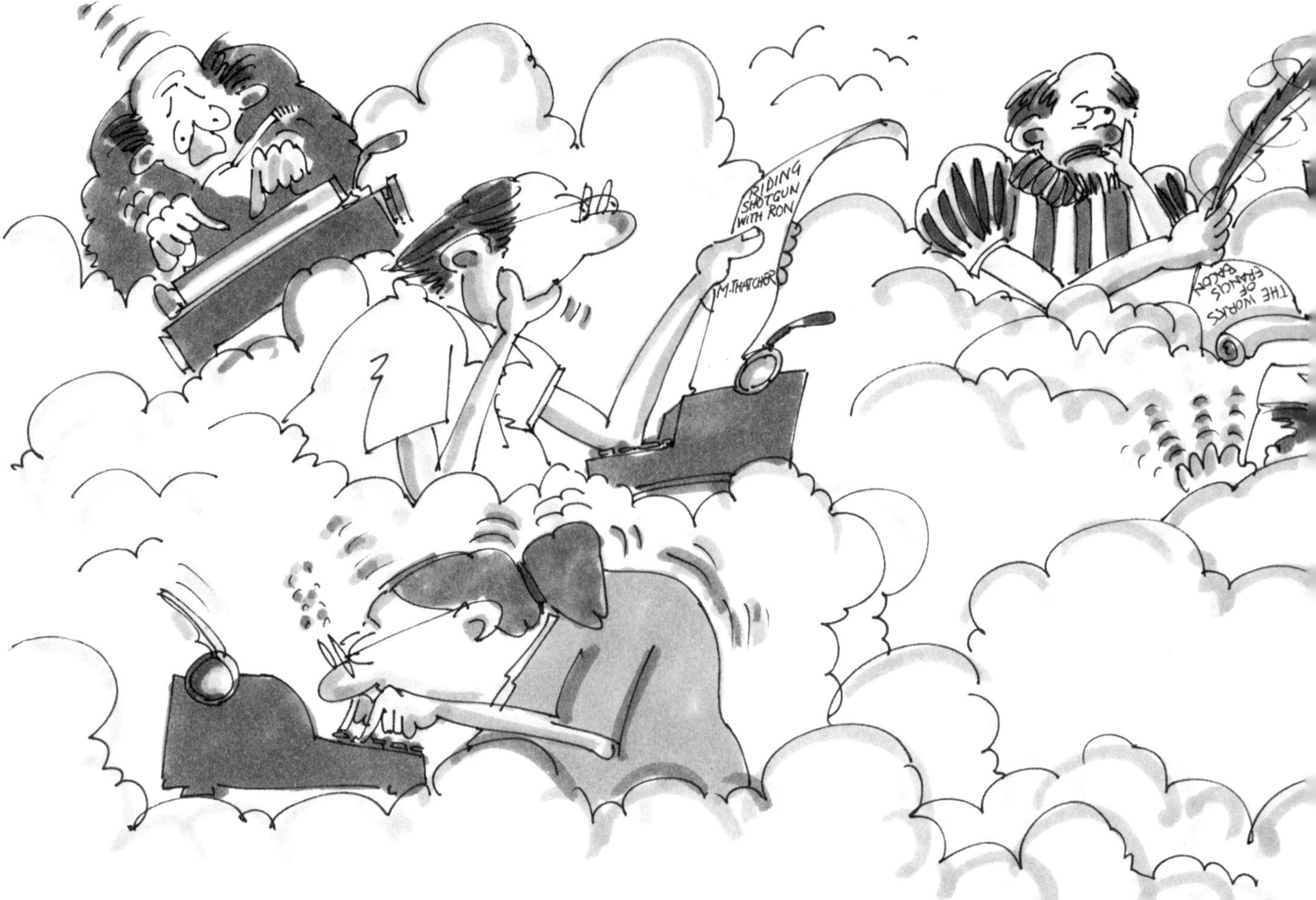
RIDING SHOTGUN WITH RON
M.THATCHER
THE WORKS OF FRANCIS BACON

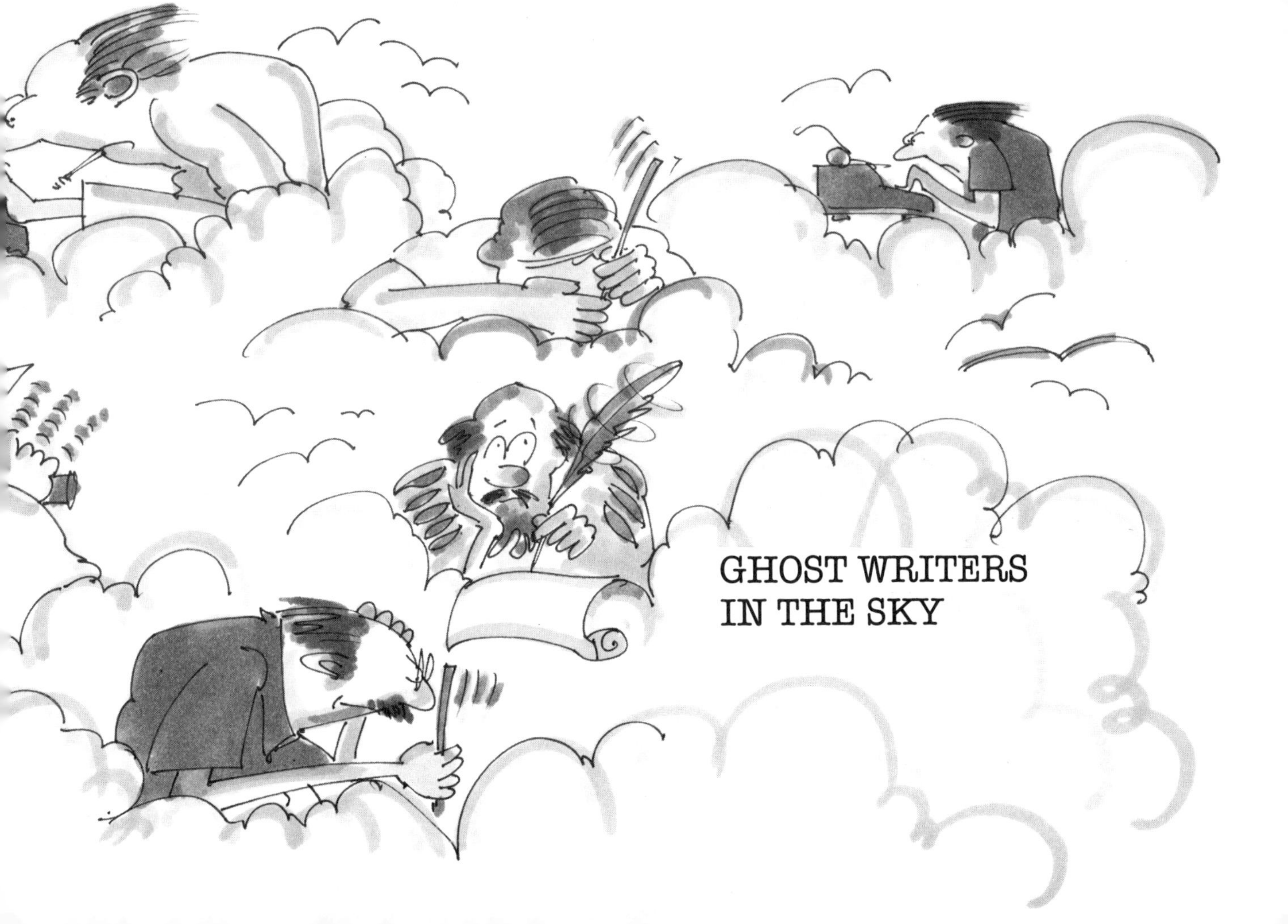

GHOST WRITERS IN THE SKY

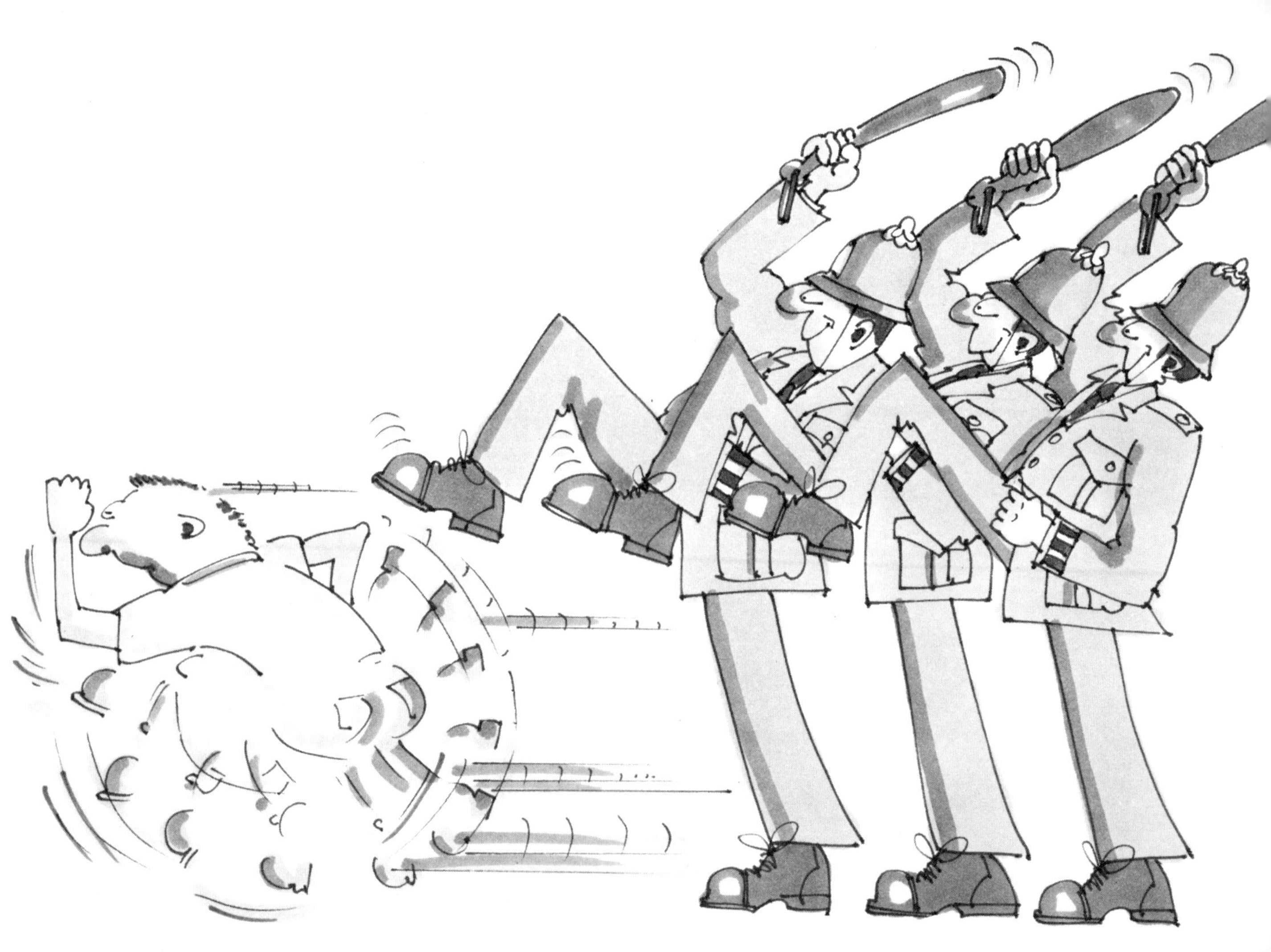

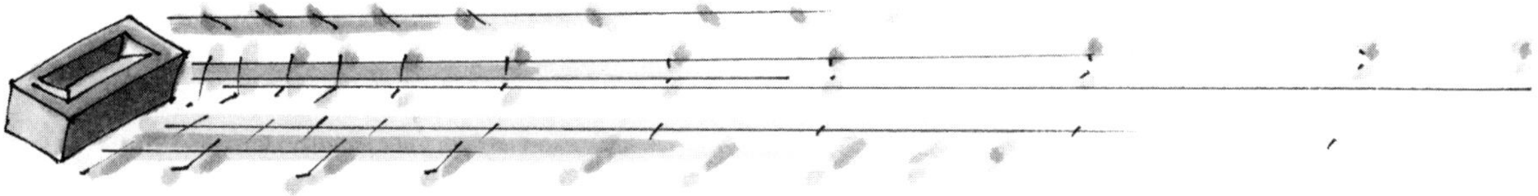

GET A YOB, SHA NA NA NA, SHA NA NA NA NA

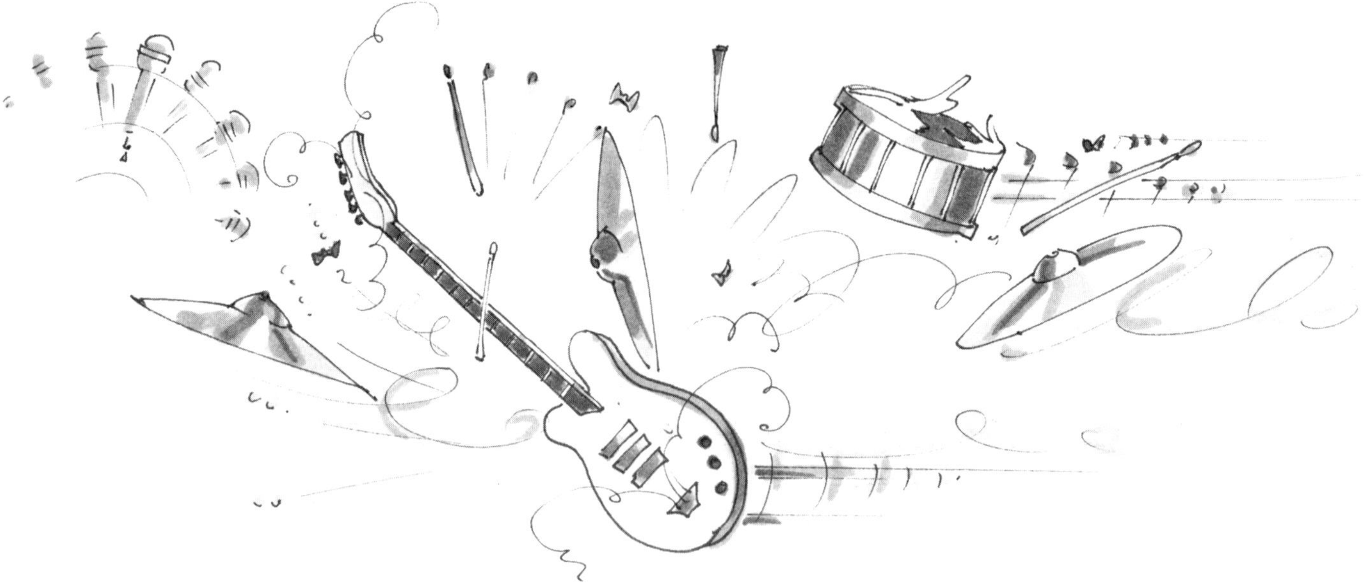

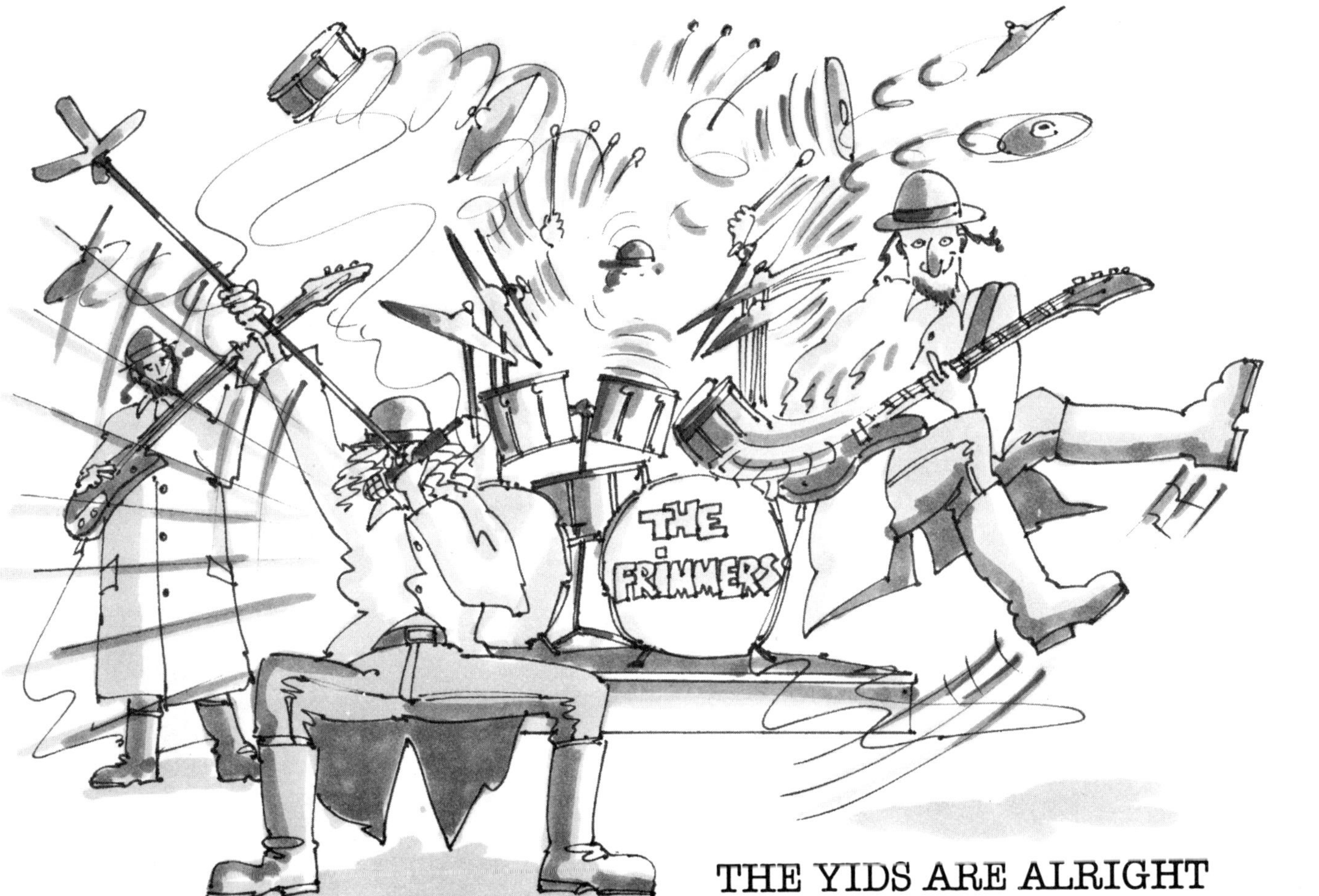

THE YIDS ARE ALRIGHT

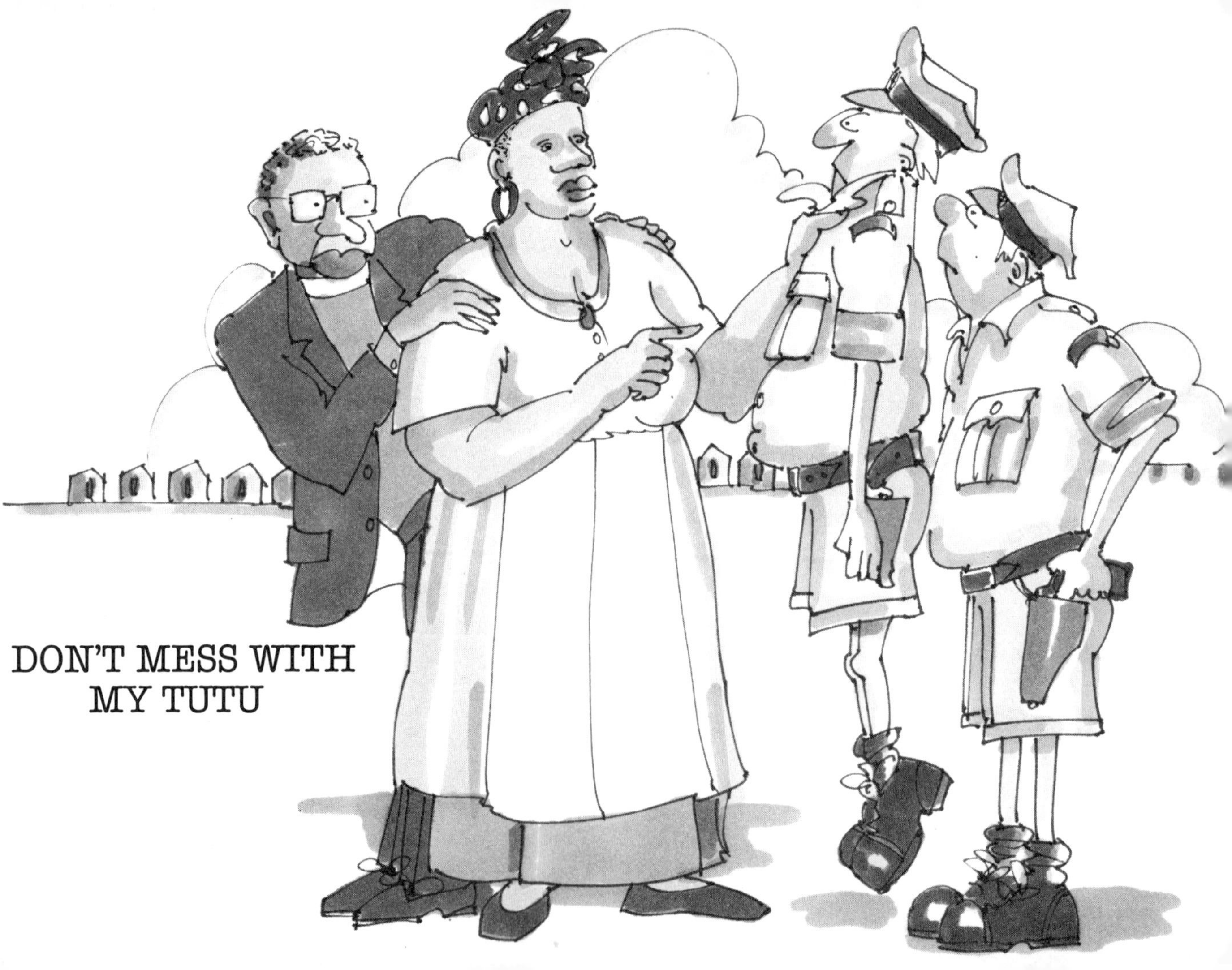

DON'T MESS WITH
MY TUTU

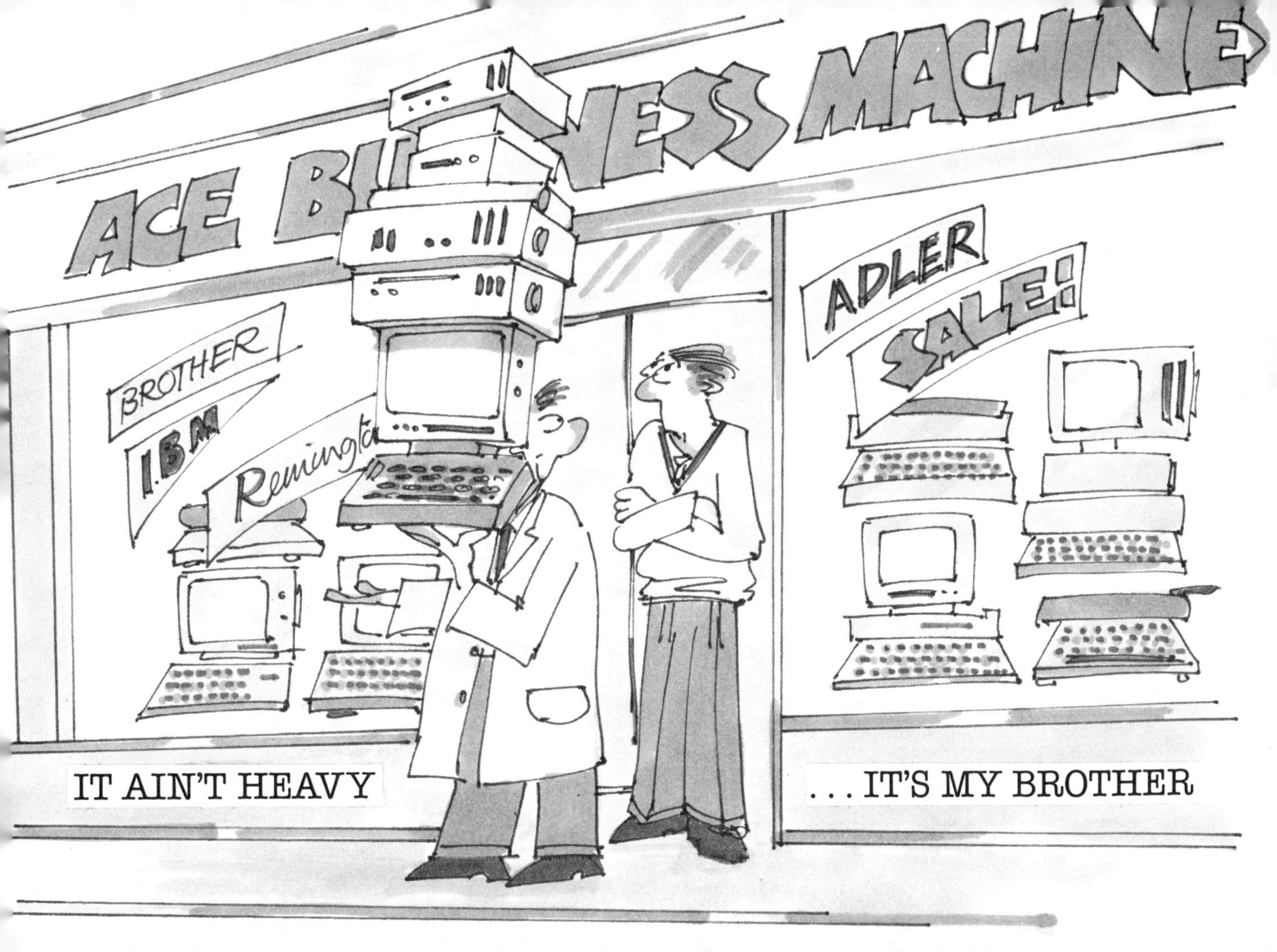

IT AIN'T HEAVY . . . IT'S MY BROTHER

I ONLY HAVE LIES FOR YOU, DEAR

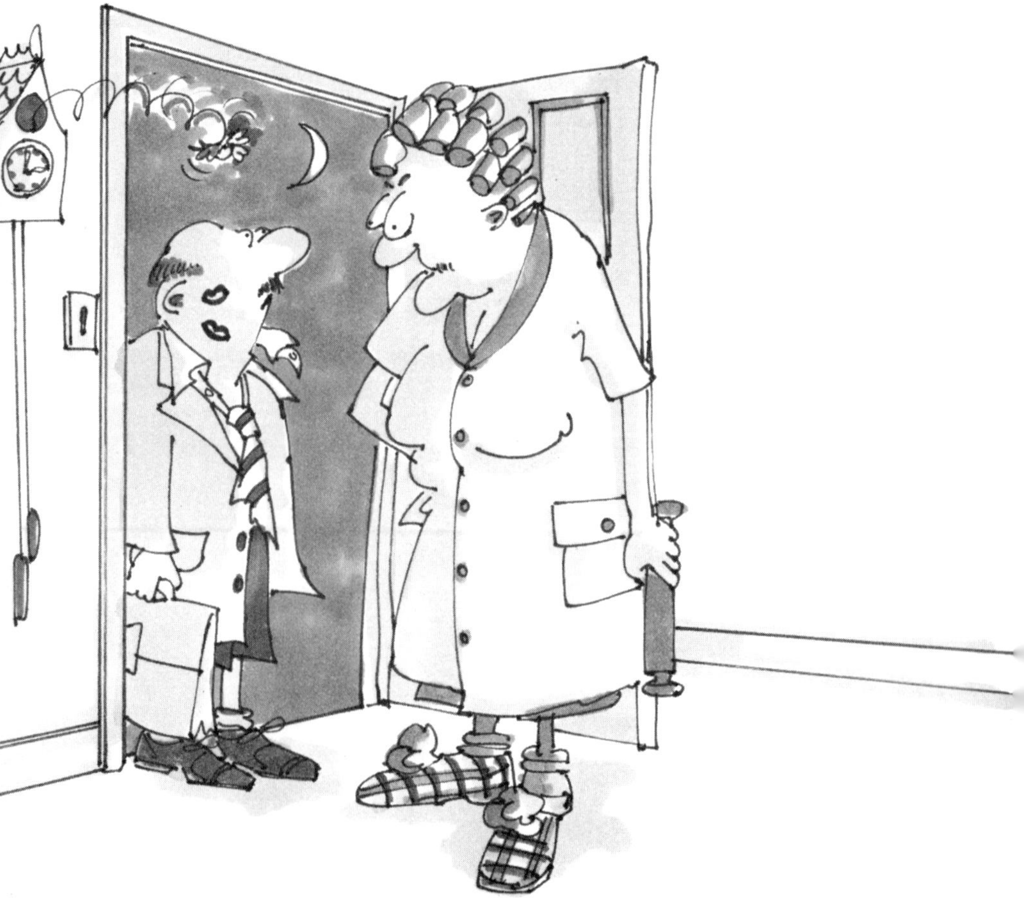

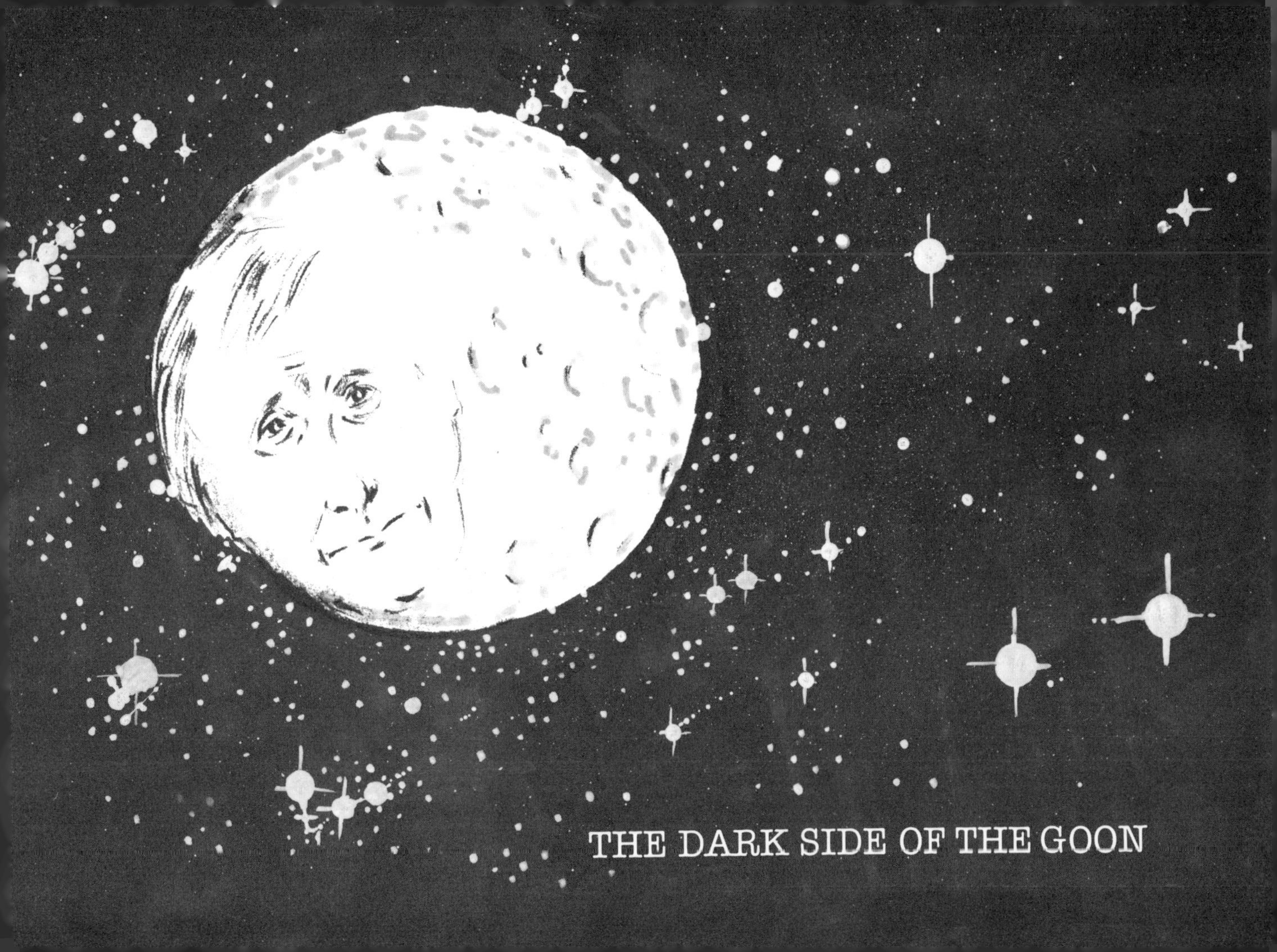

THE DARK SIDE OF THE GOON

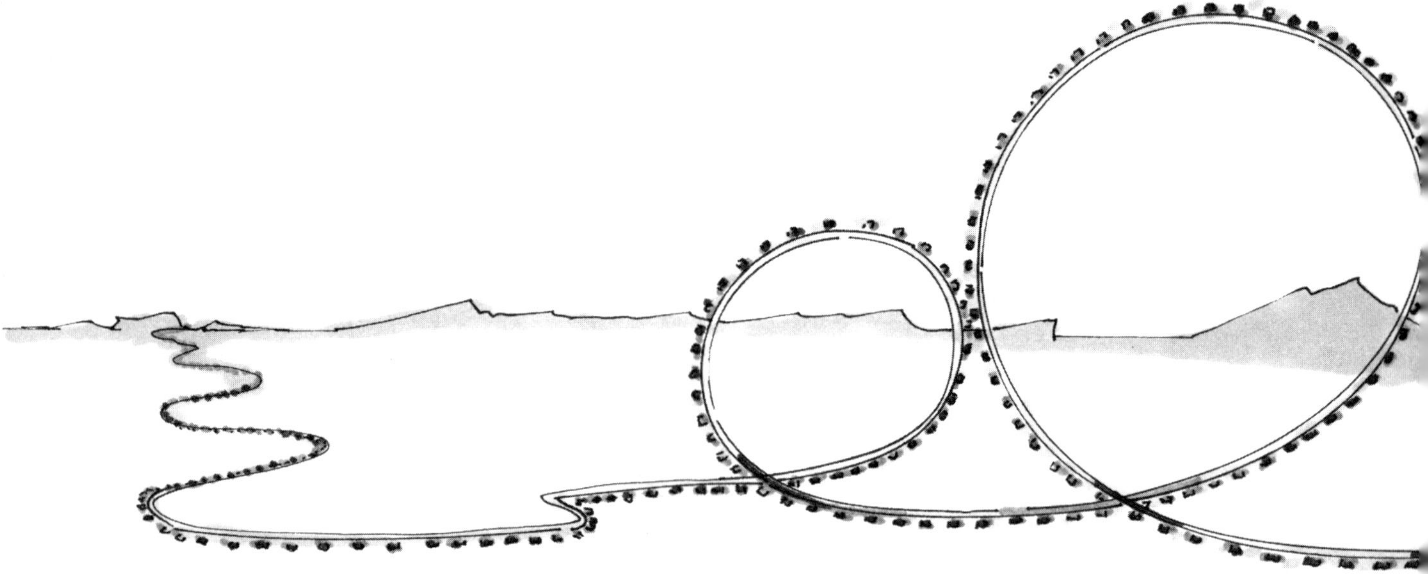

DO THE LOCO MOTION WITH ME

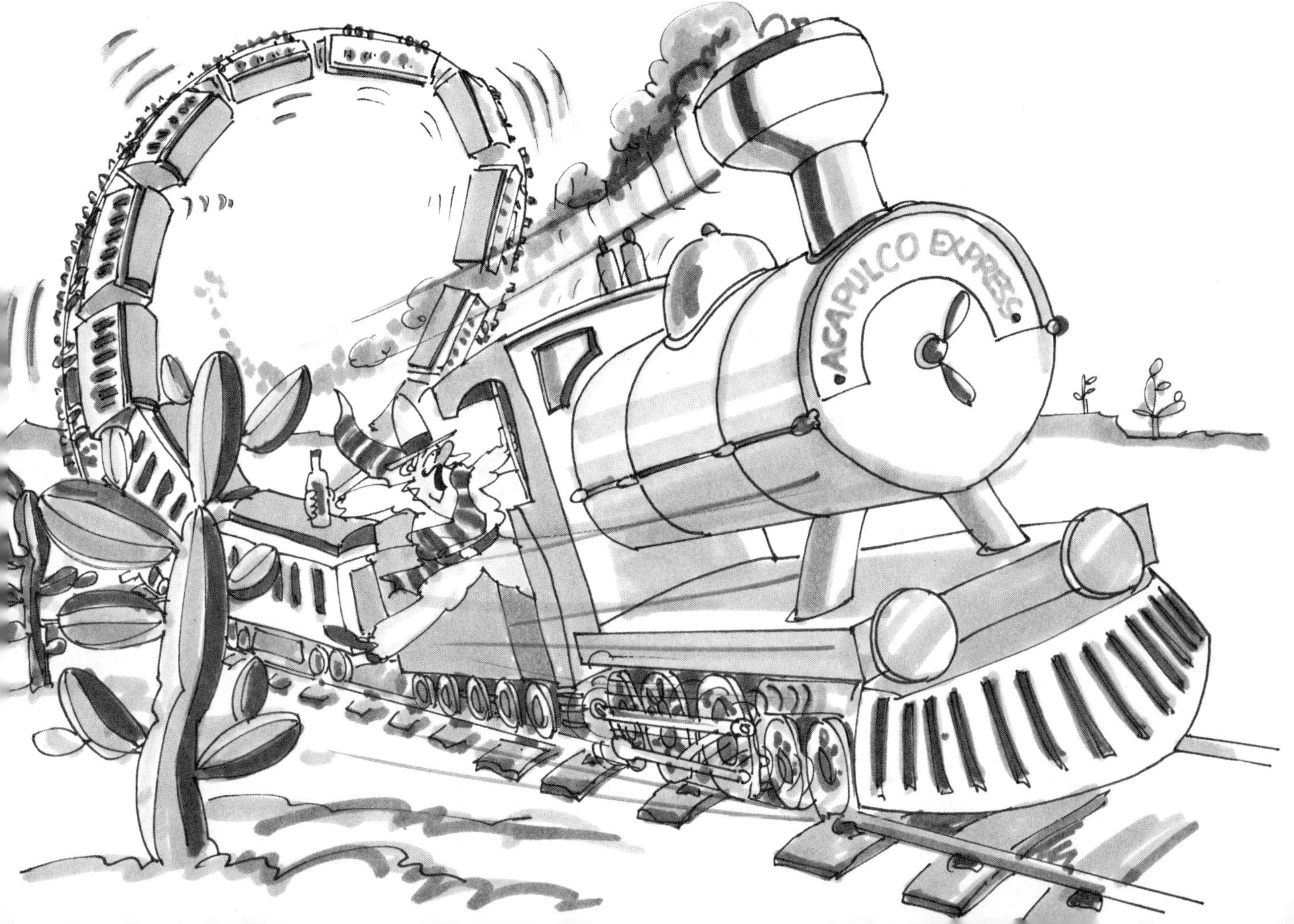
ACAPULCO EXPRESS

PUTTING ON THE BLITZ

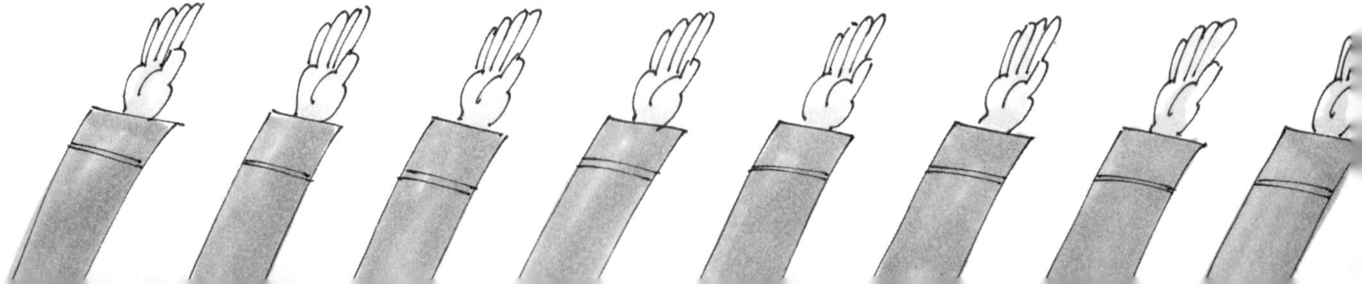

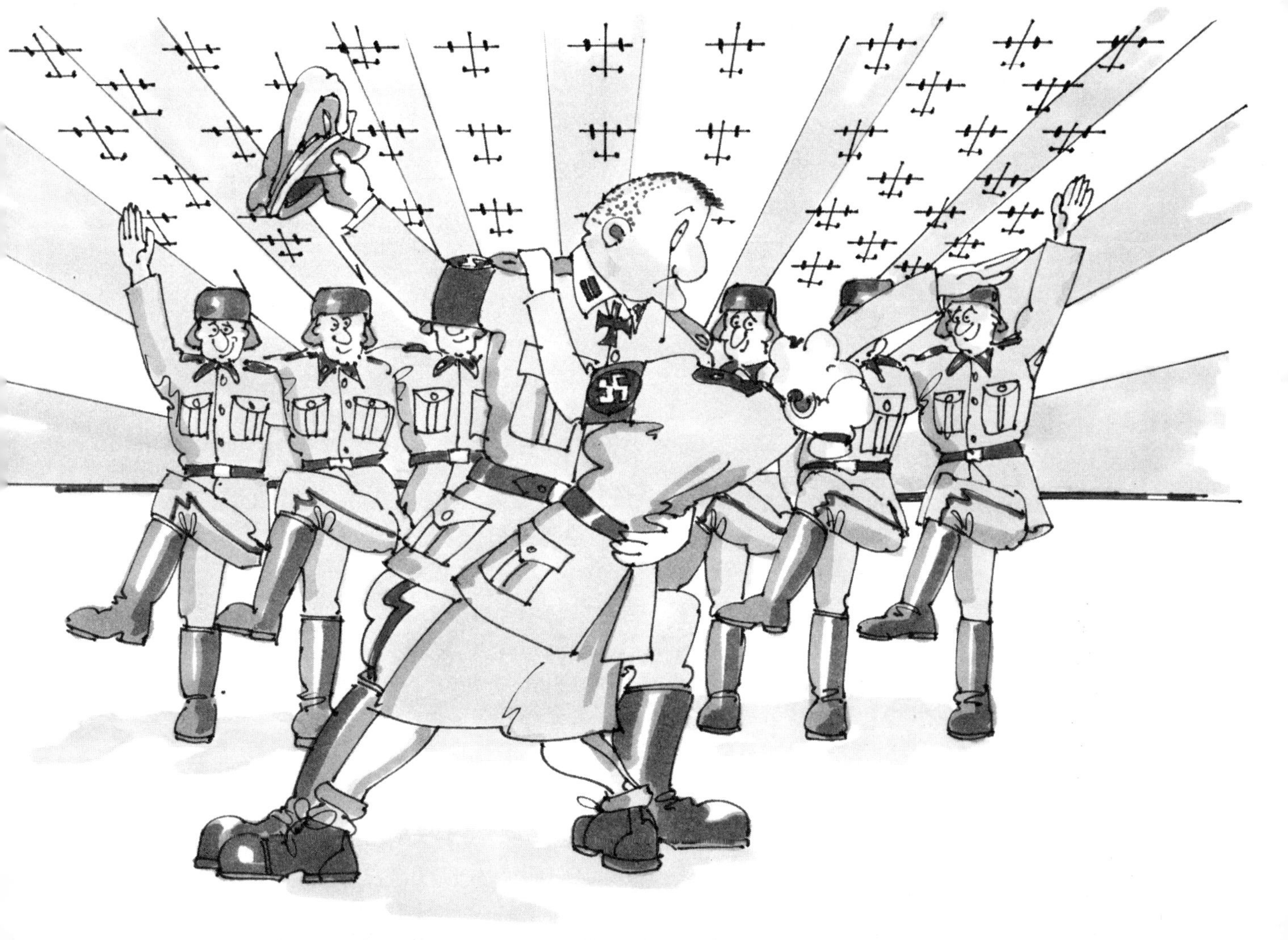

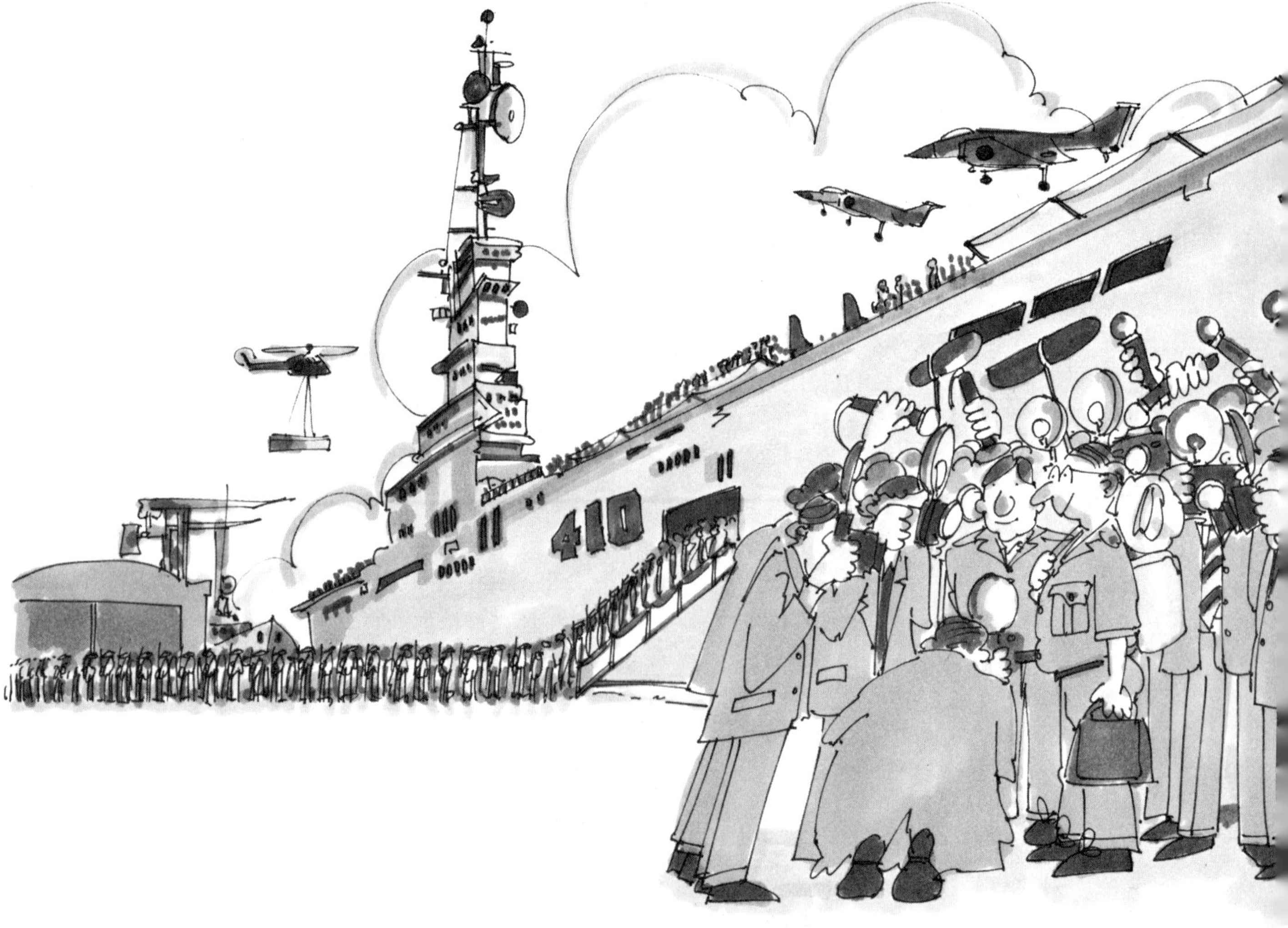
410

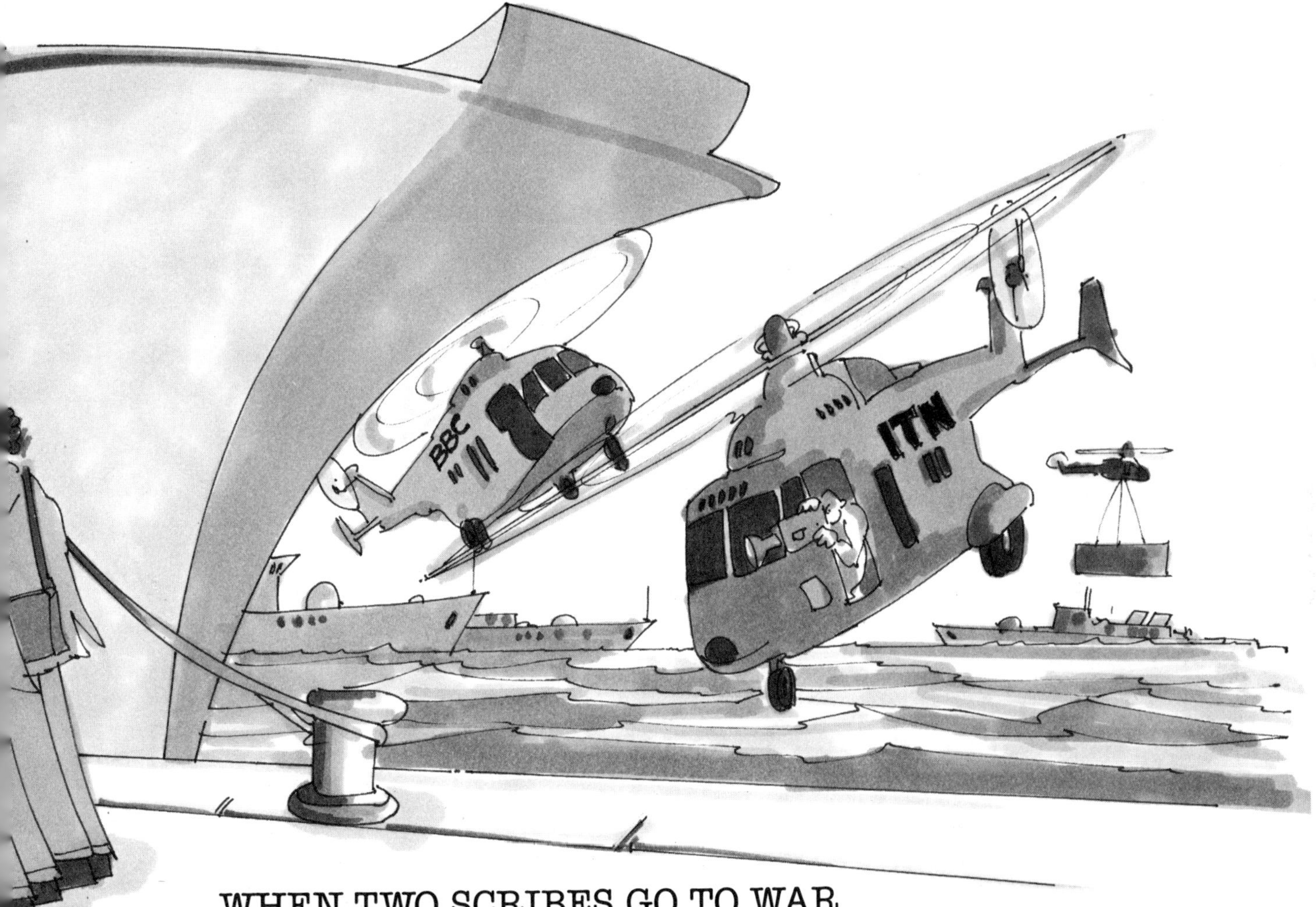

WHEN TWO SCRIBES GO TO WAR

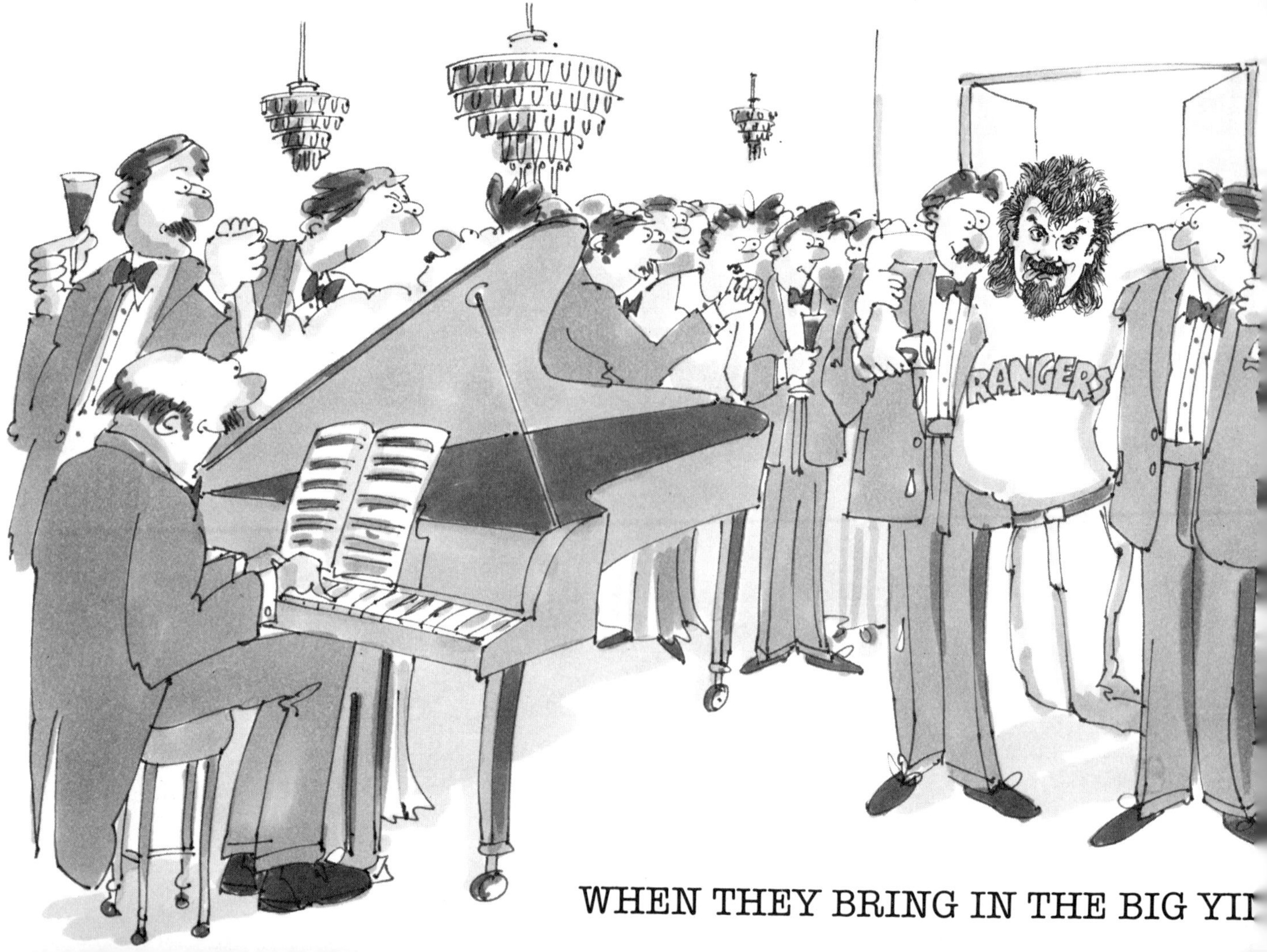

WHEN THEY BRING IN THE BIG YI

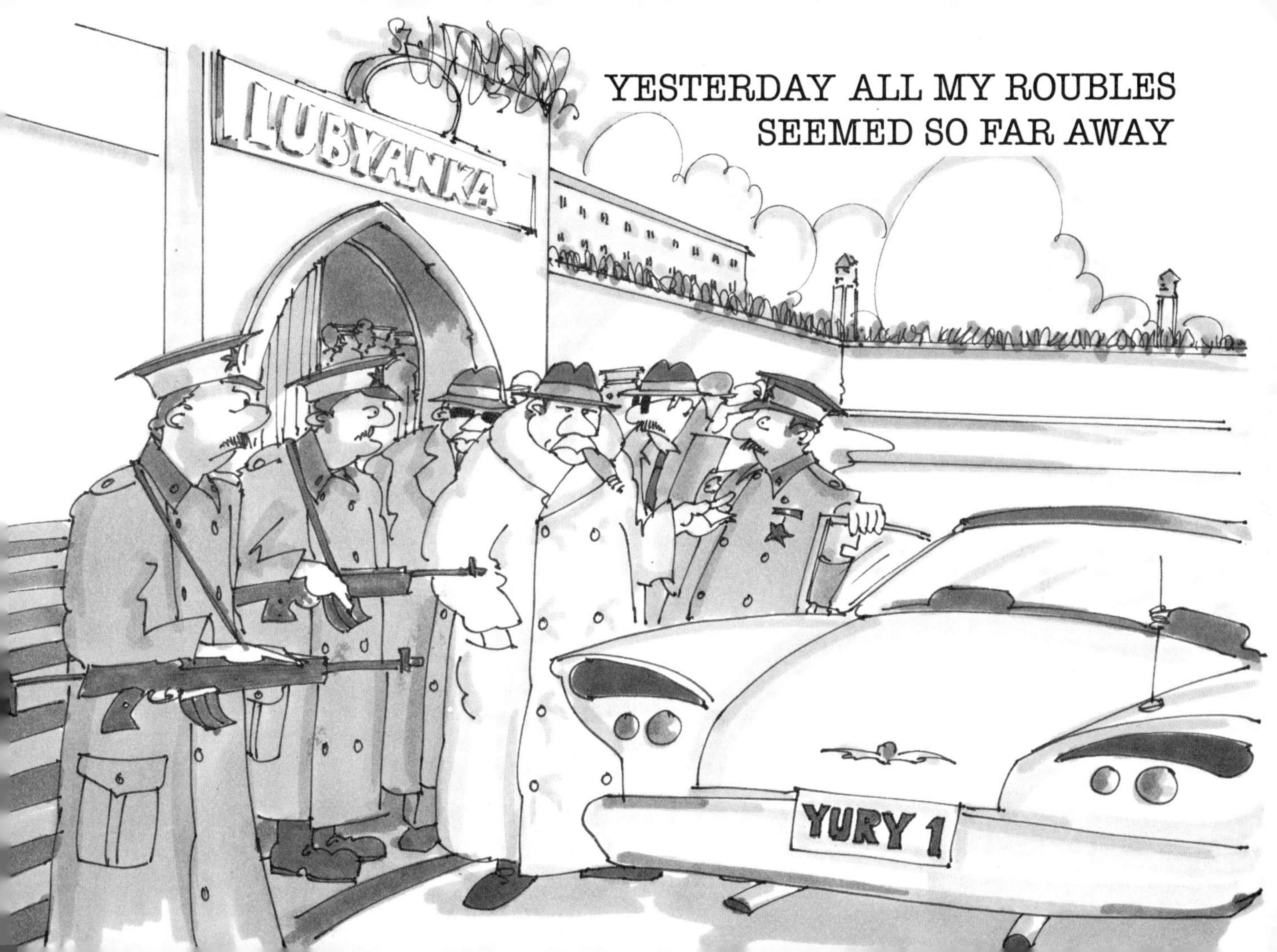
YESTERDAY ALL MY ROUBLES
SEEMED SO FAR AWAY
LUBYANKA
YURY 1

MY SWEET LARD

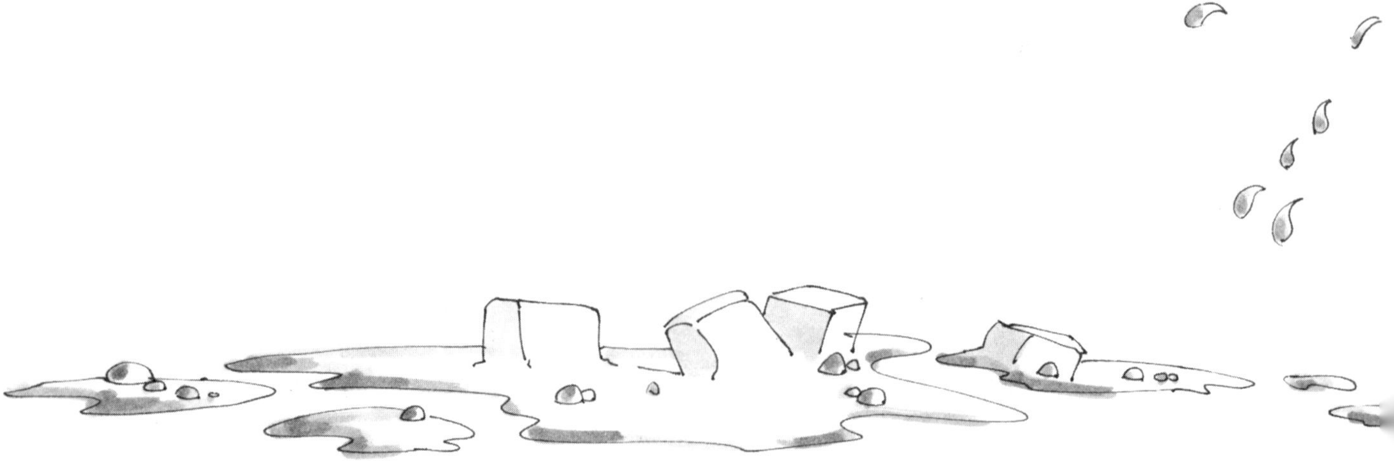

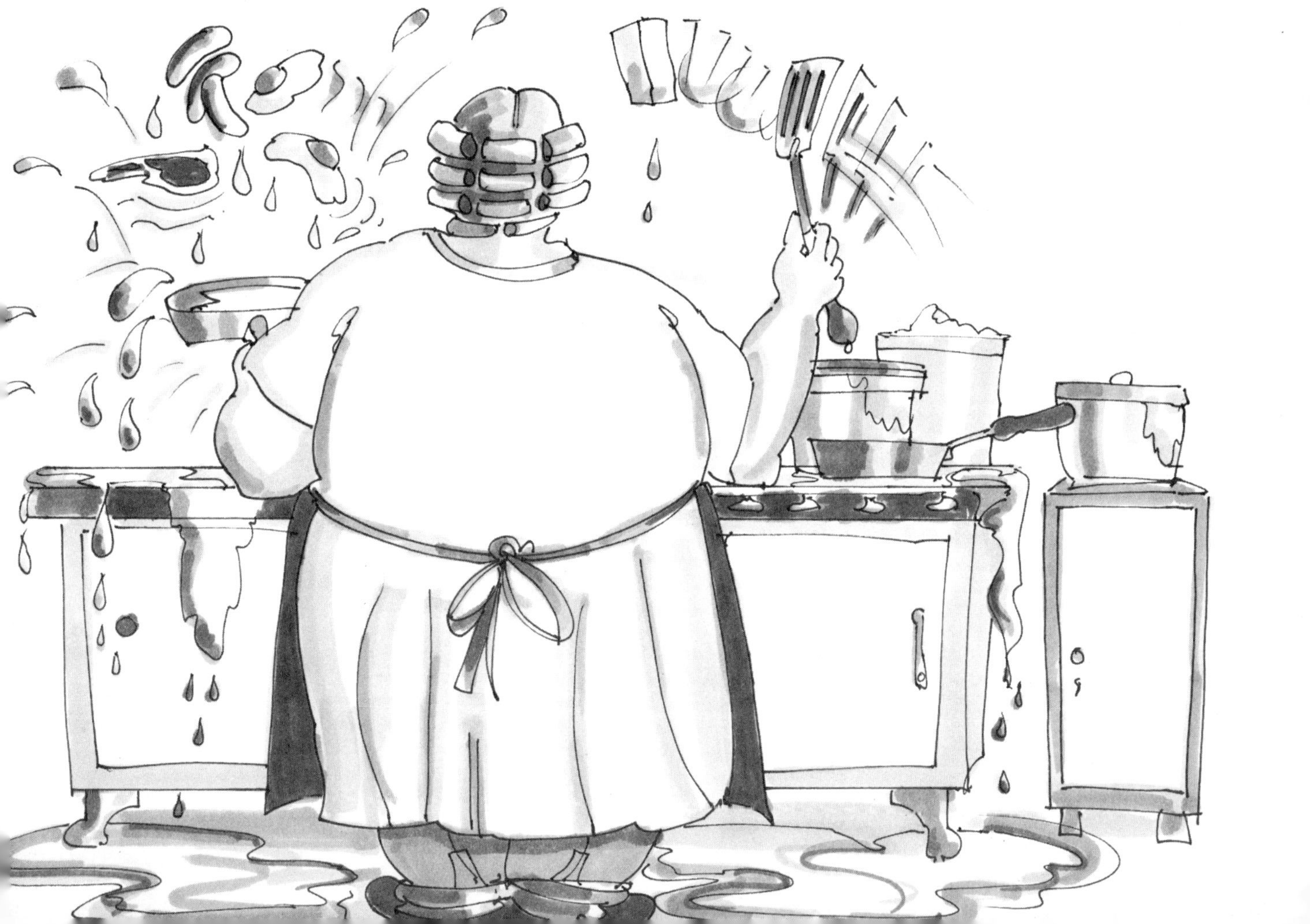

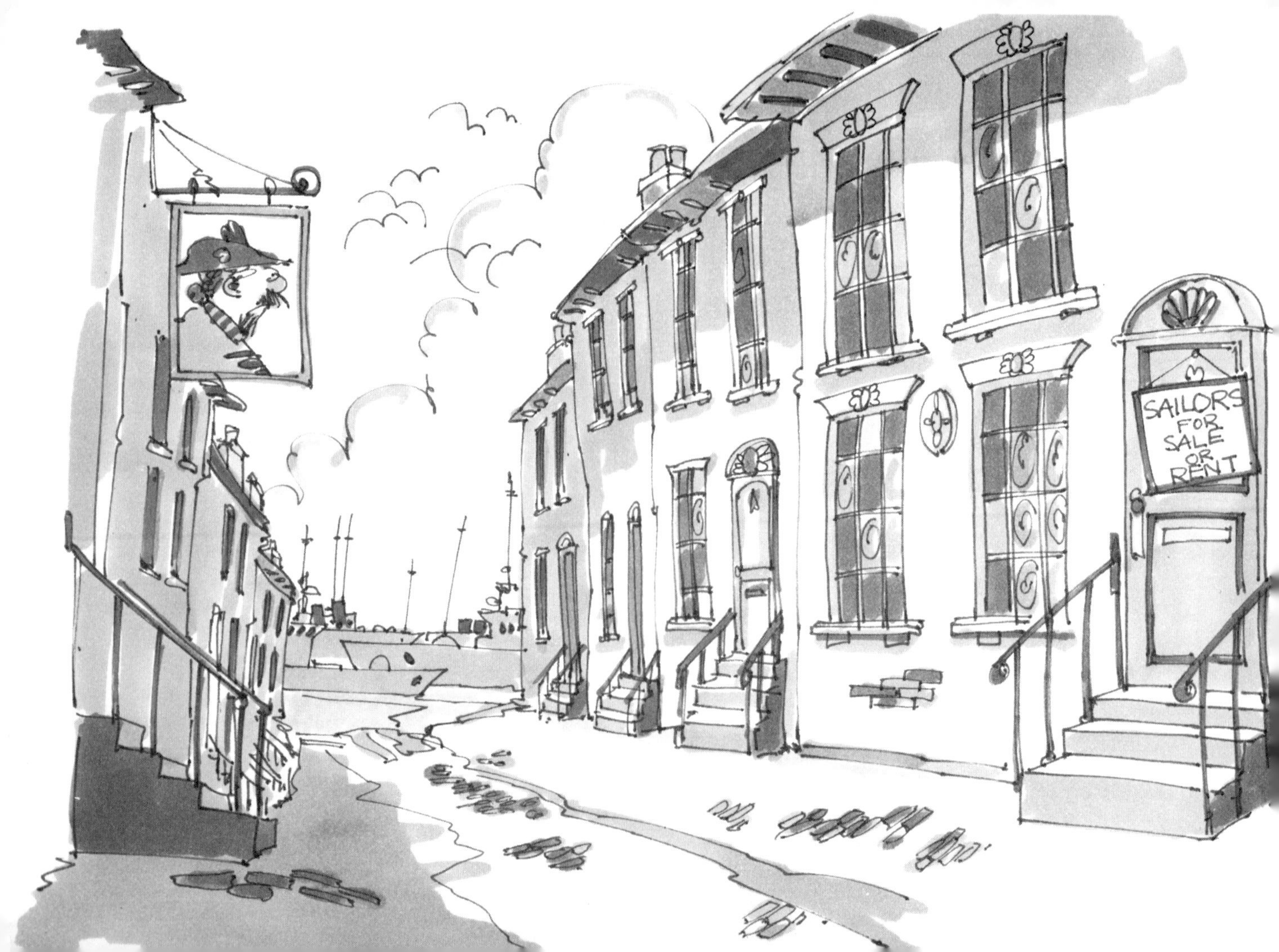
SAILORS FOR SALE OR RENT

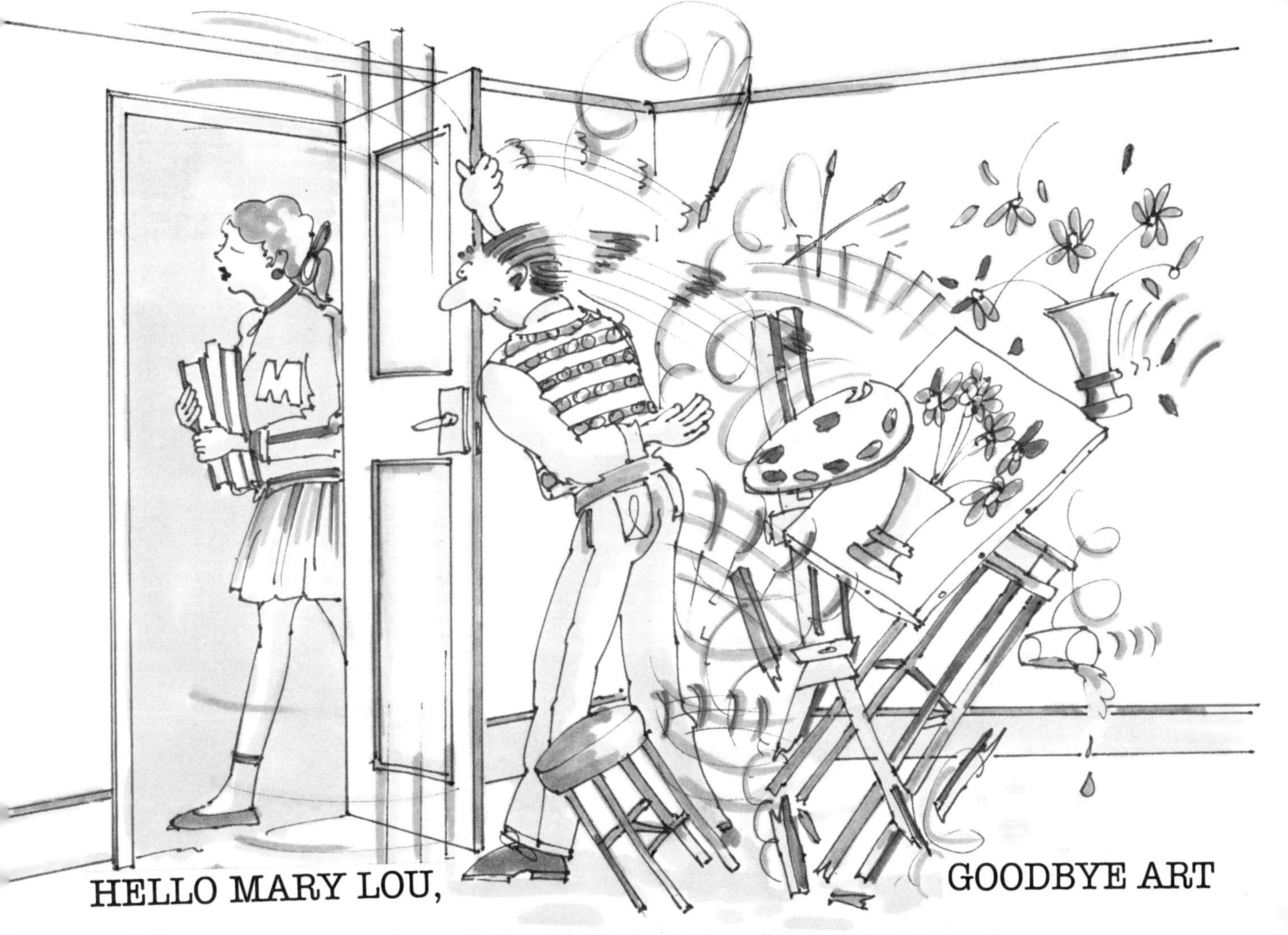

HELLO MARY LOU, GOODBYE ART

THE MINUTE YOU WALKED IN THE JOINT, I COULD TELL YOU WERE A MAN OF EXTINCTION

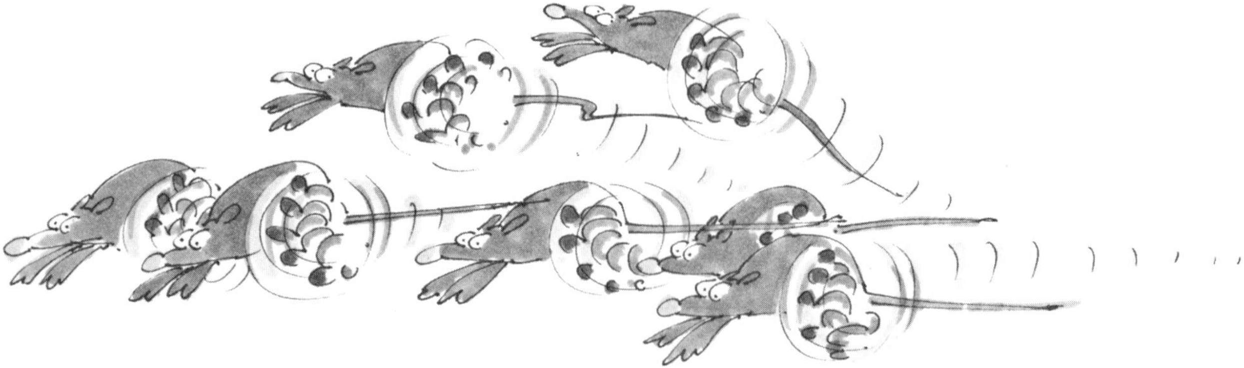

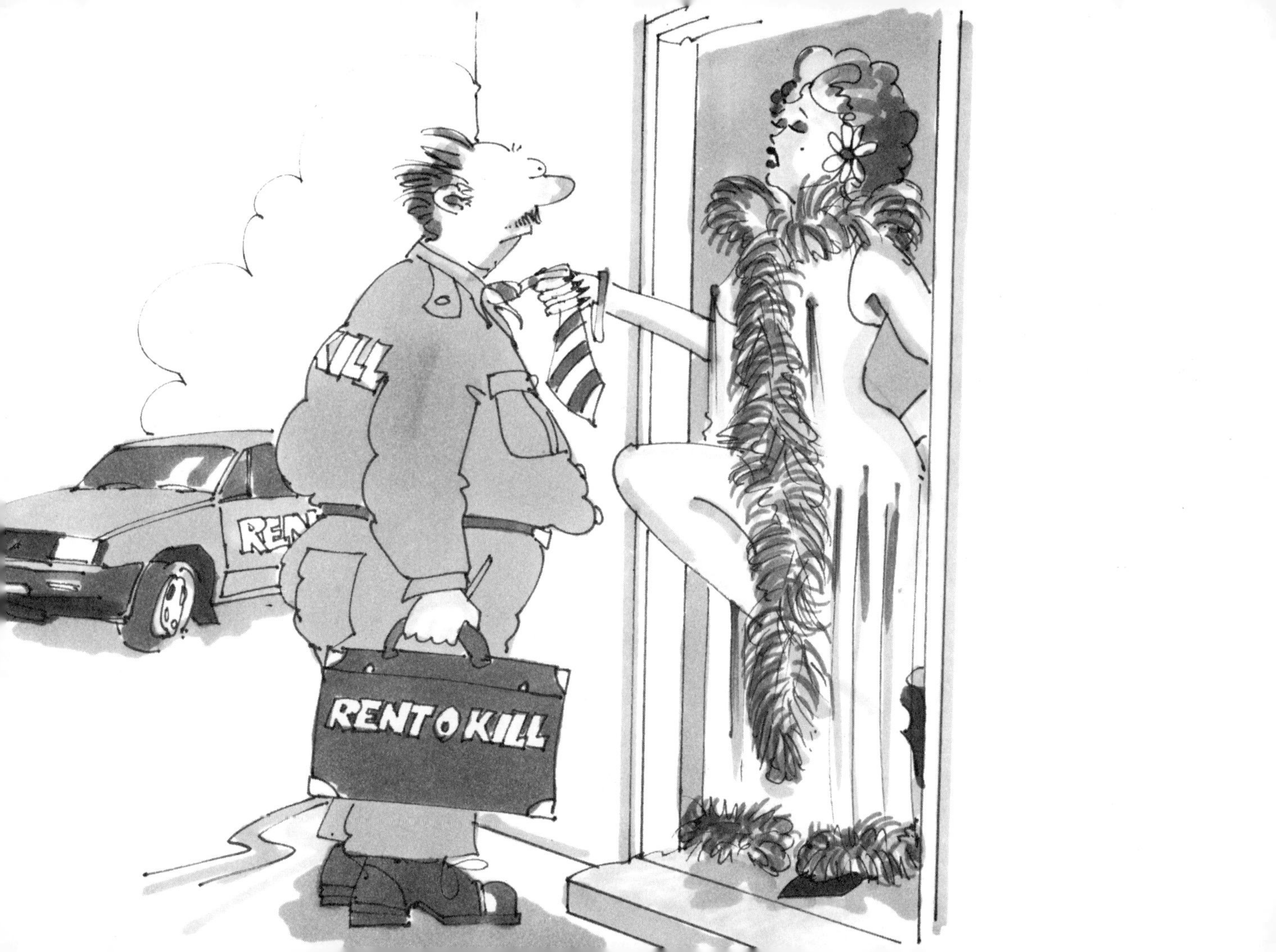
KILL
RENT O KILL

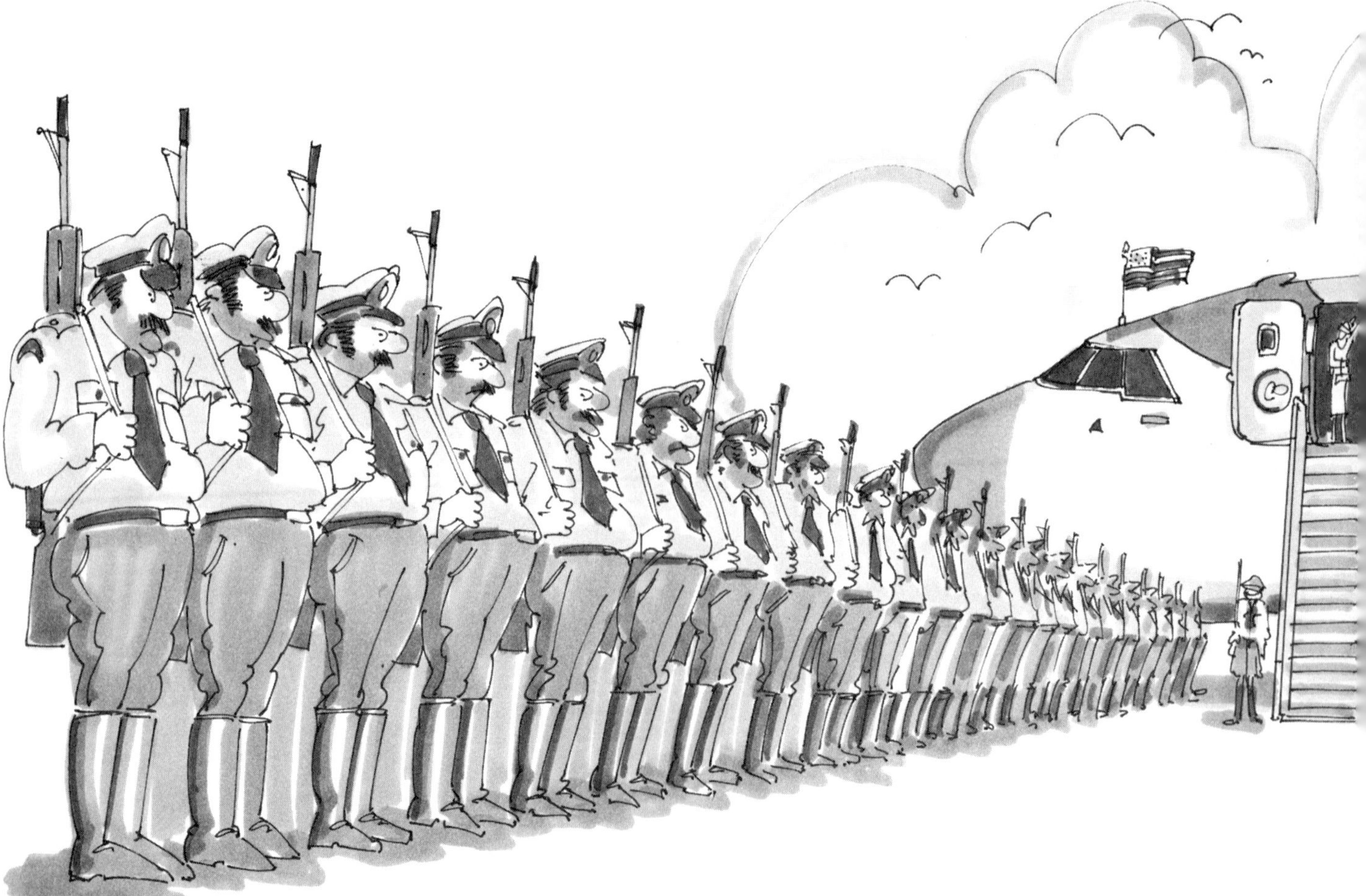

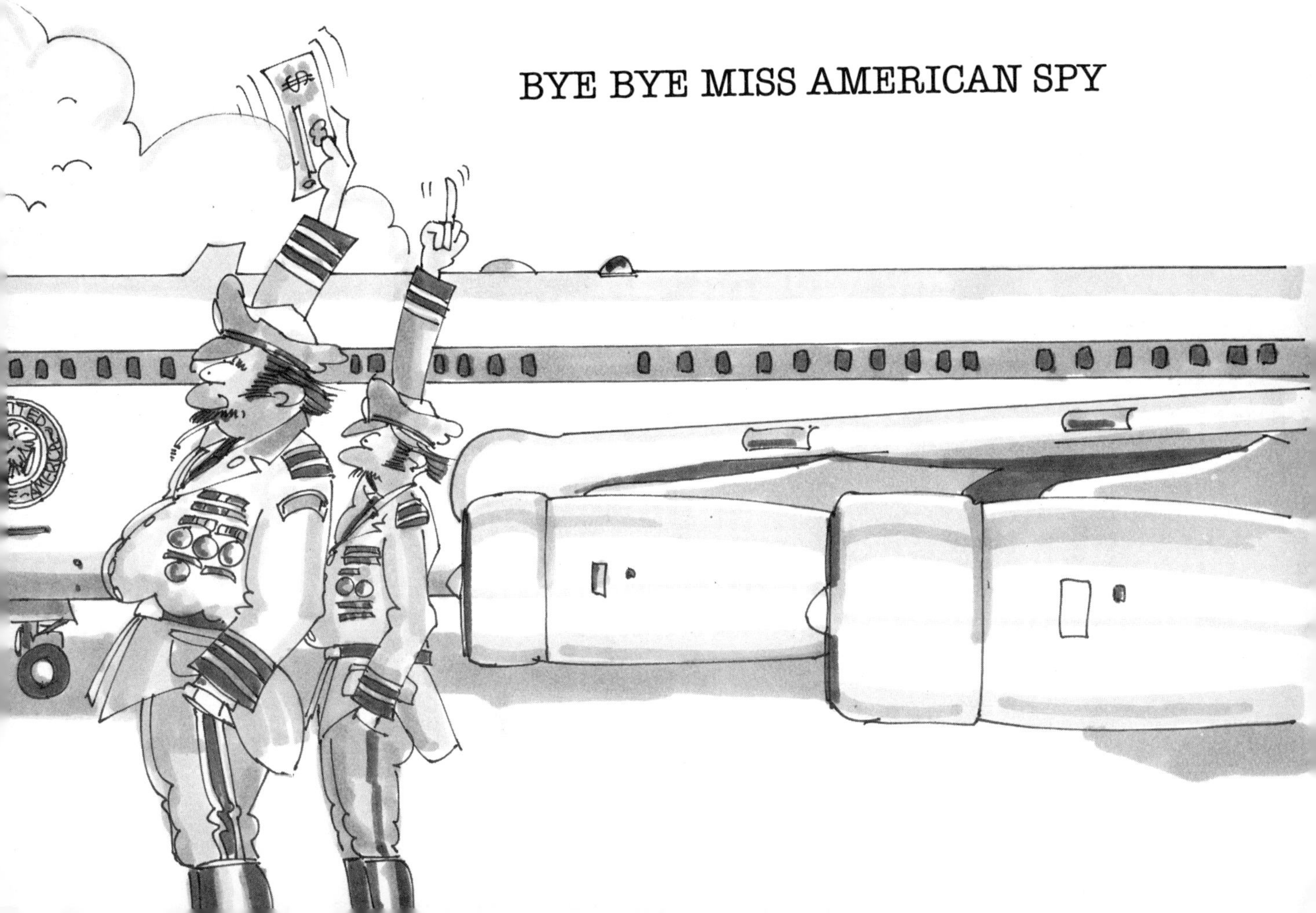

BYE BYE MISS AMERICAN SPY

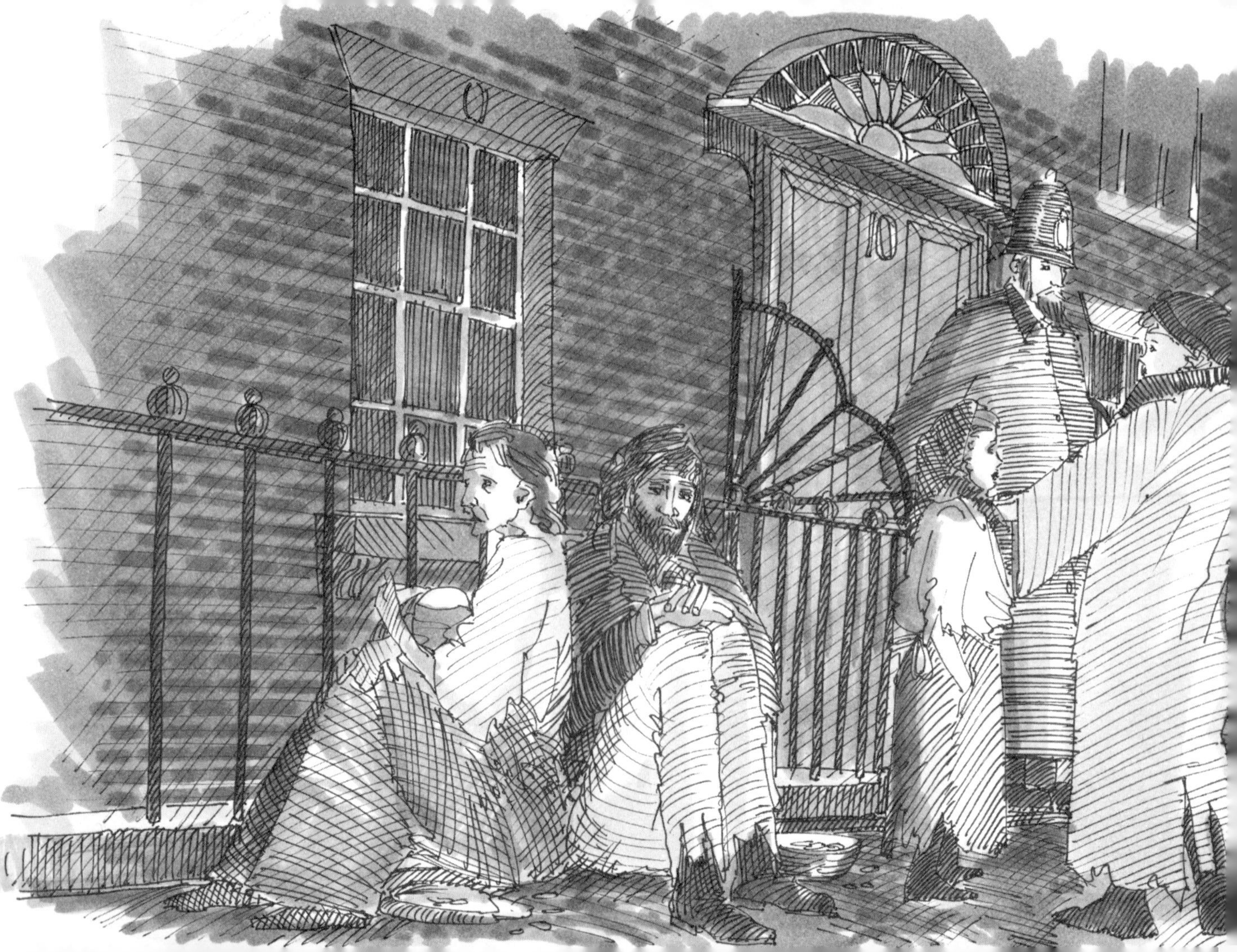
10

WE'LL EAT MEAT AGAIN, DON'T KNOW WHERE,
DON'T KNOW WHEN

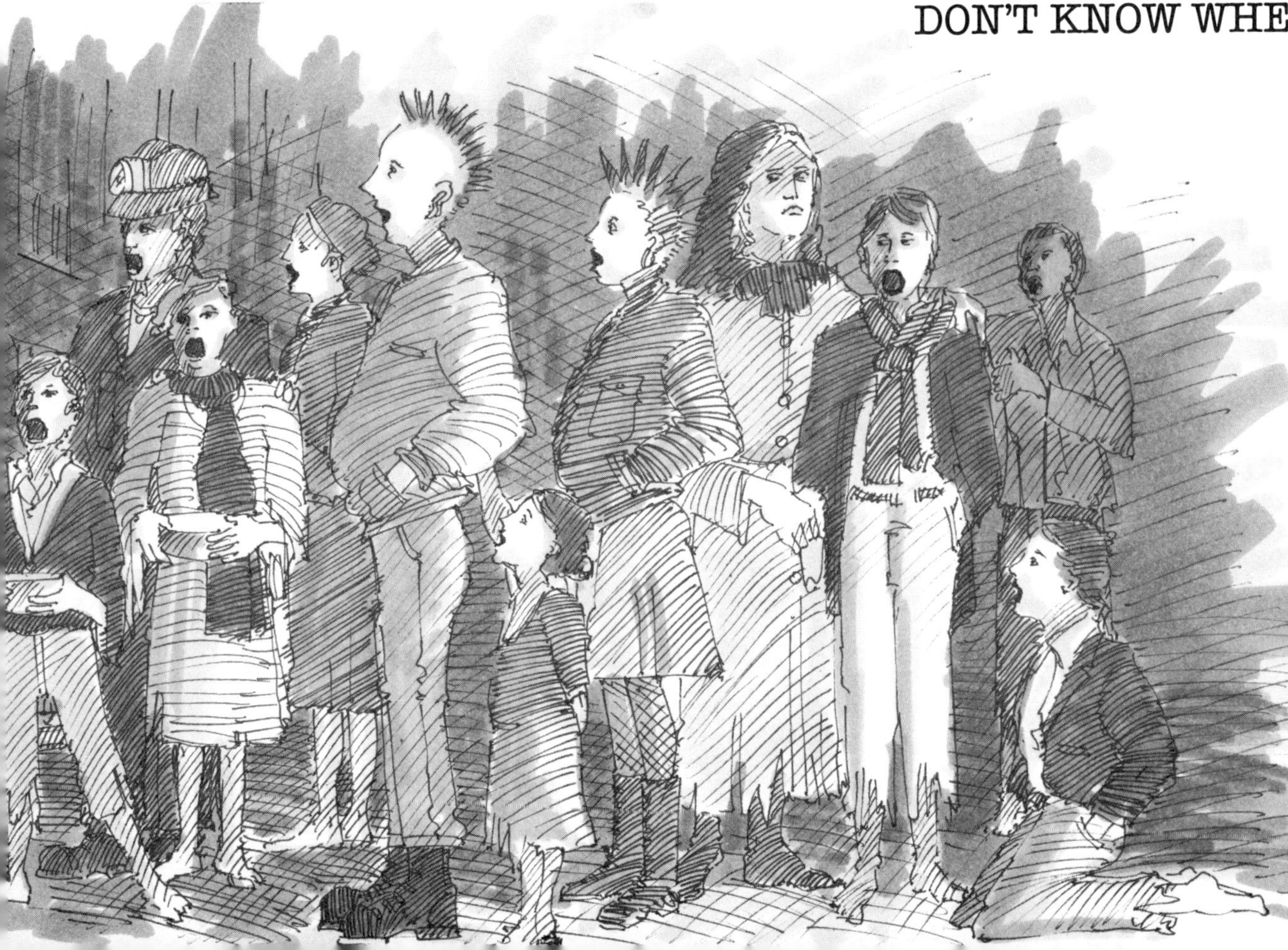

RUDOLPH THE RED KNOWS RAIN DEAR

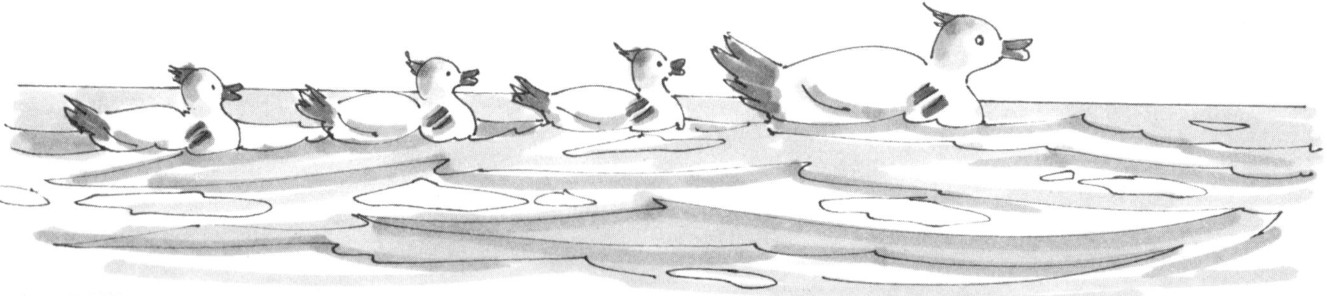

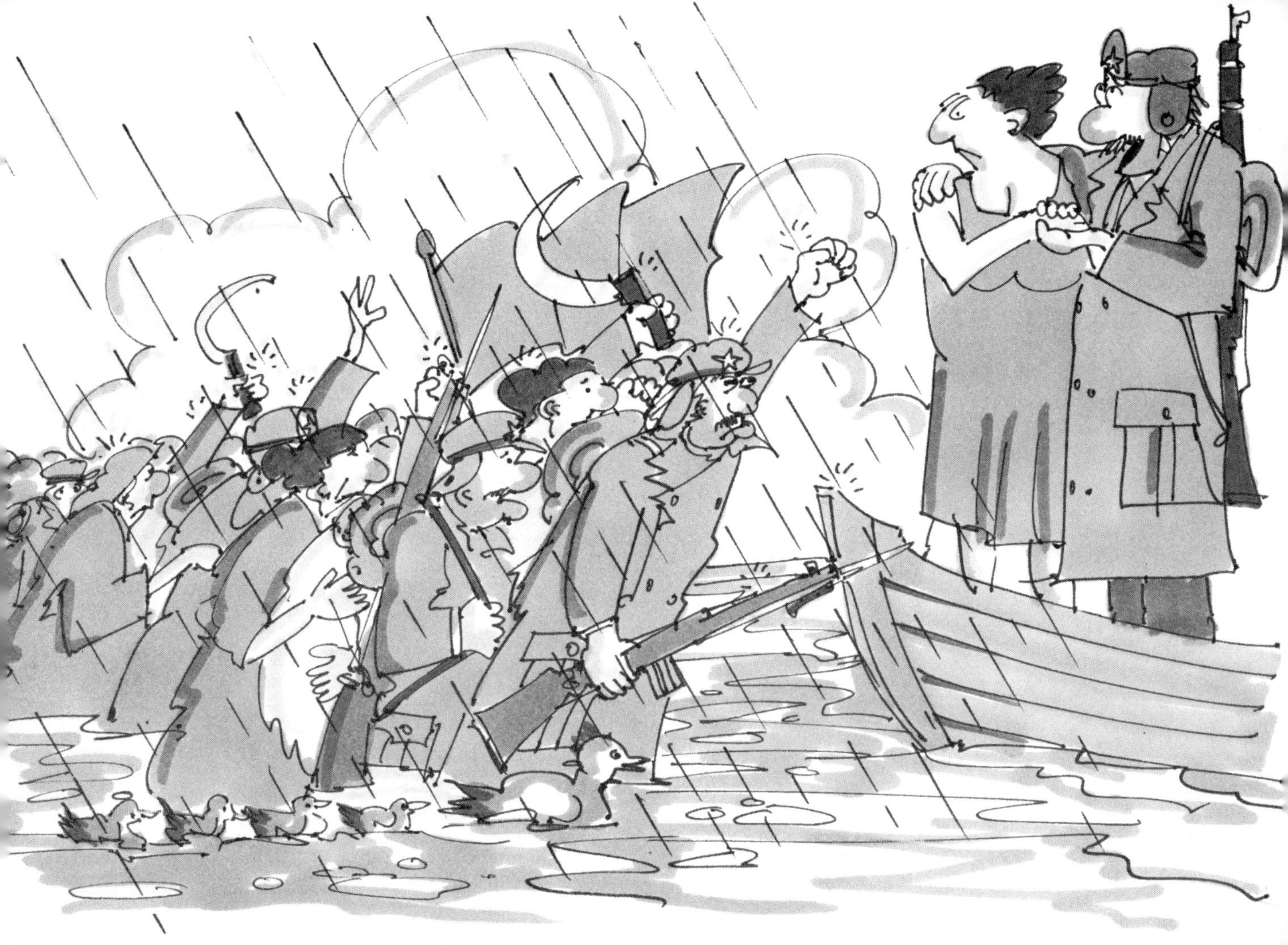

TWO SPANISH FLIES

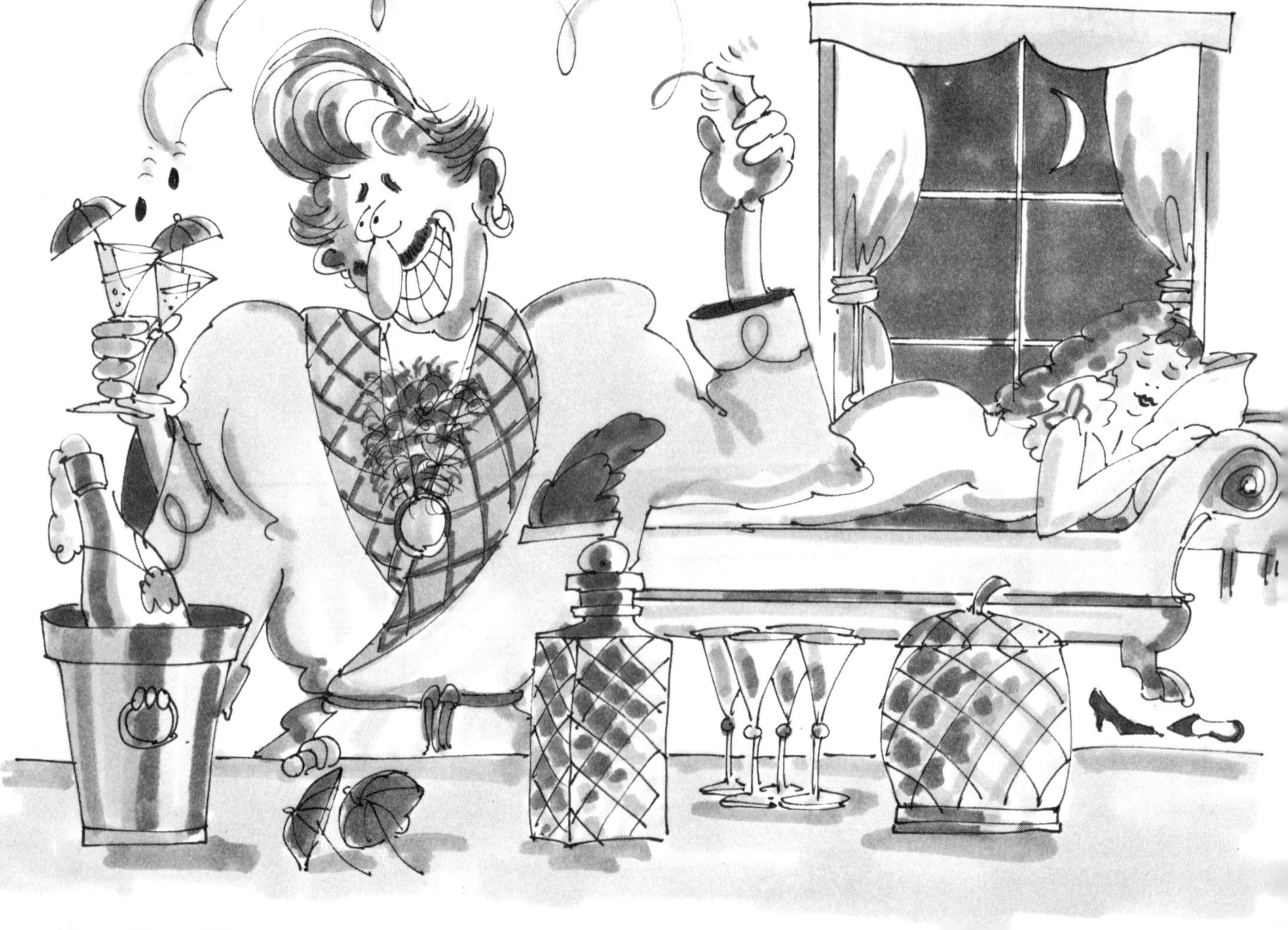

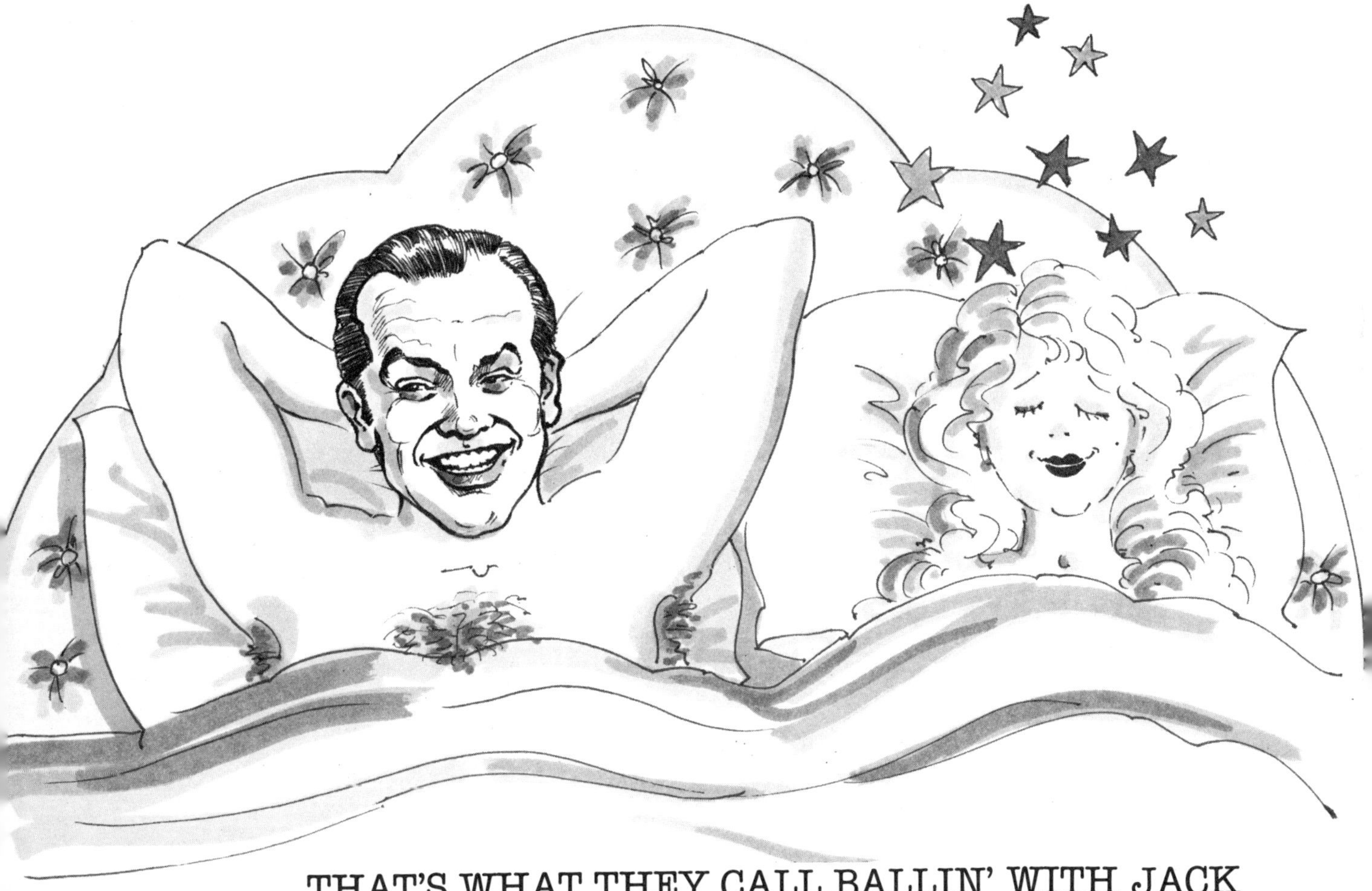

THAT'S WHAT THEY CALL BALLIN' WITH JACK

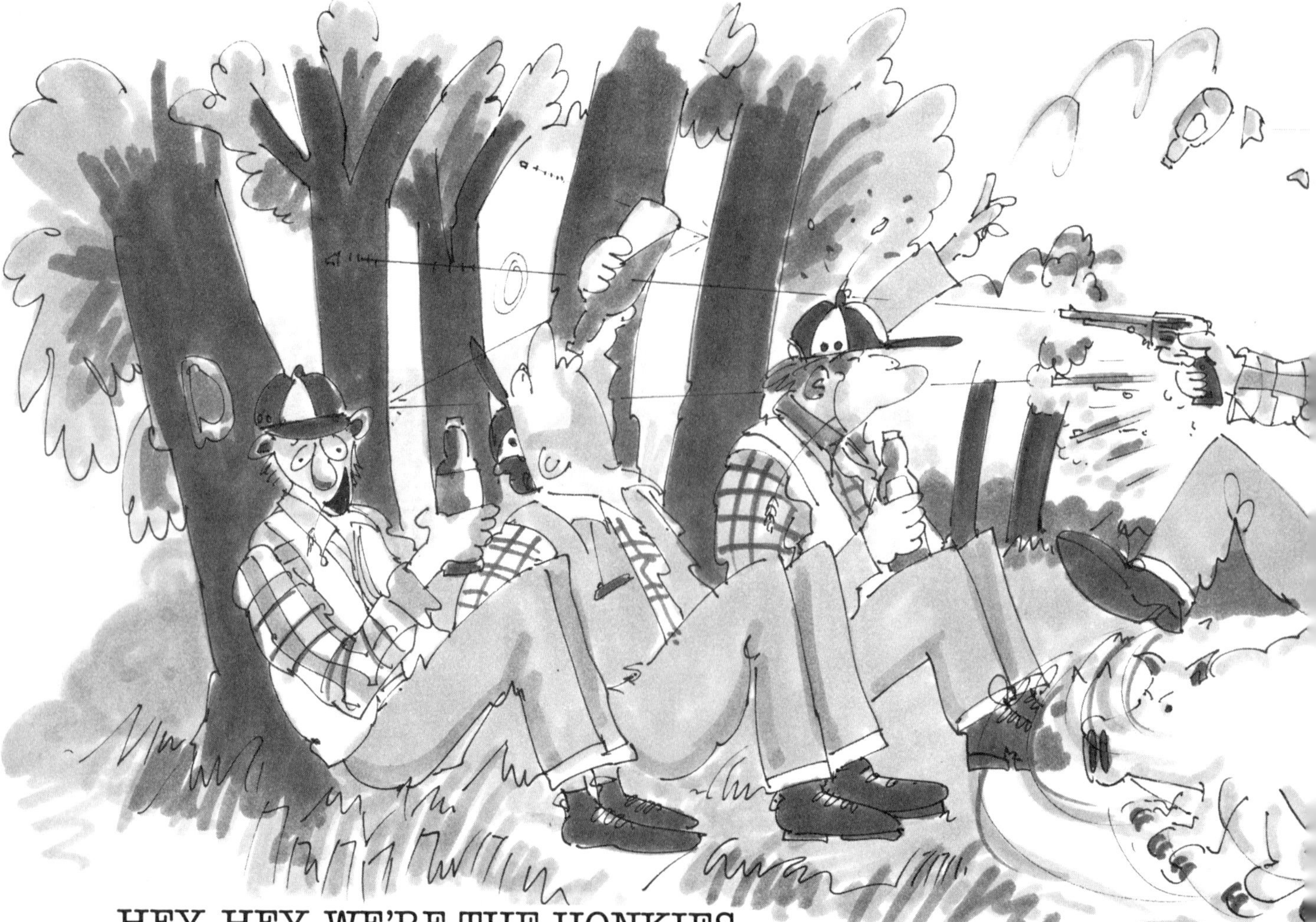

HEY, HEY, WE'RE THE HONKIES

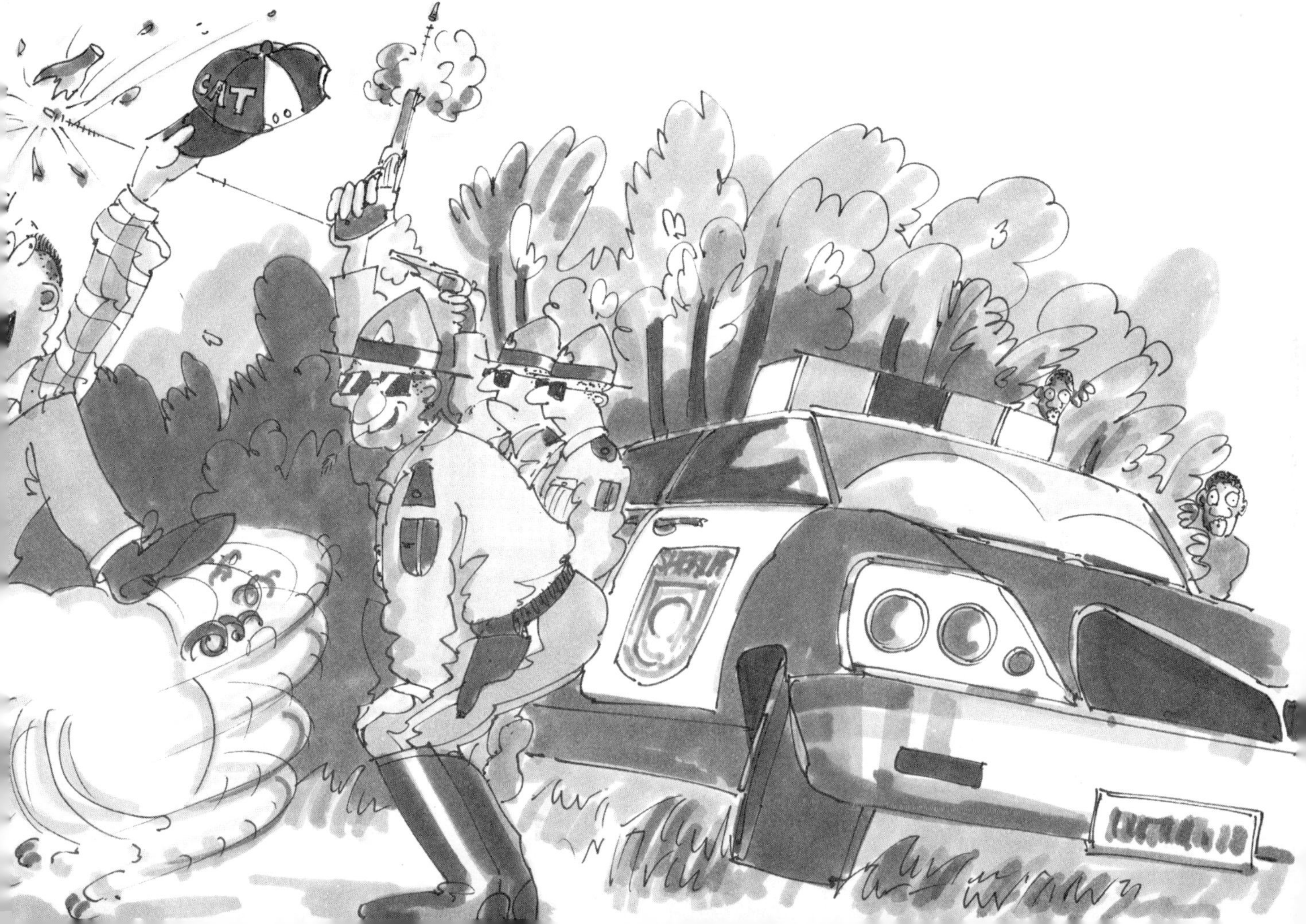
CAT

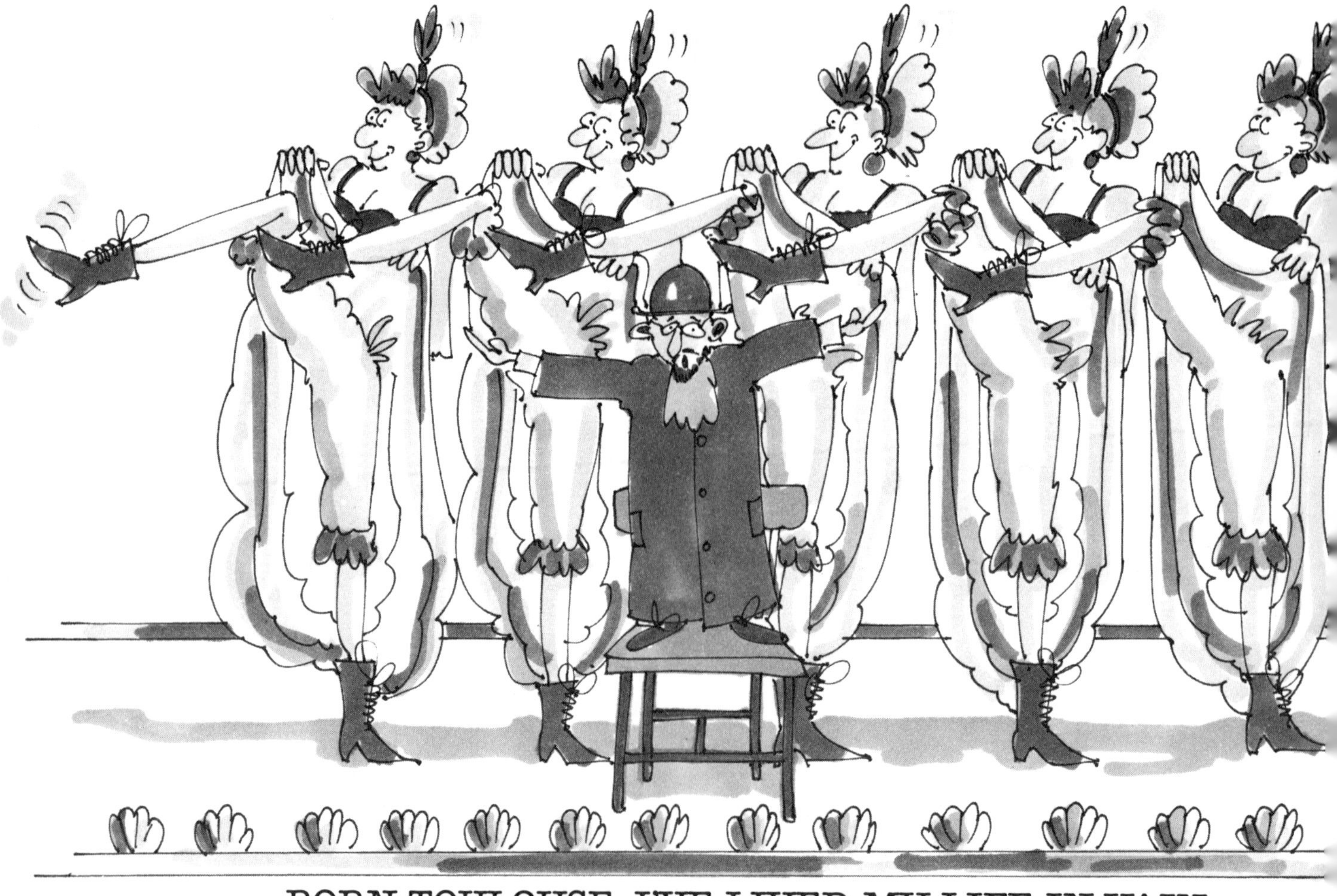

BORN TOULOUSE, I'VE LIVED MY LIFE IN VAIN

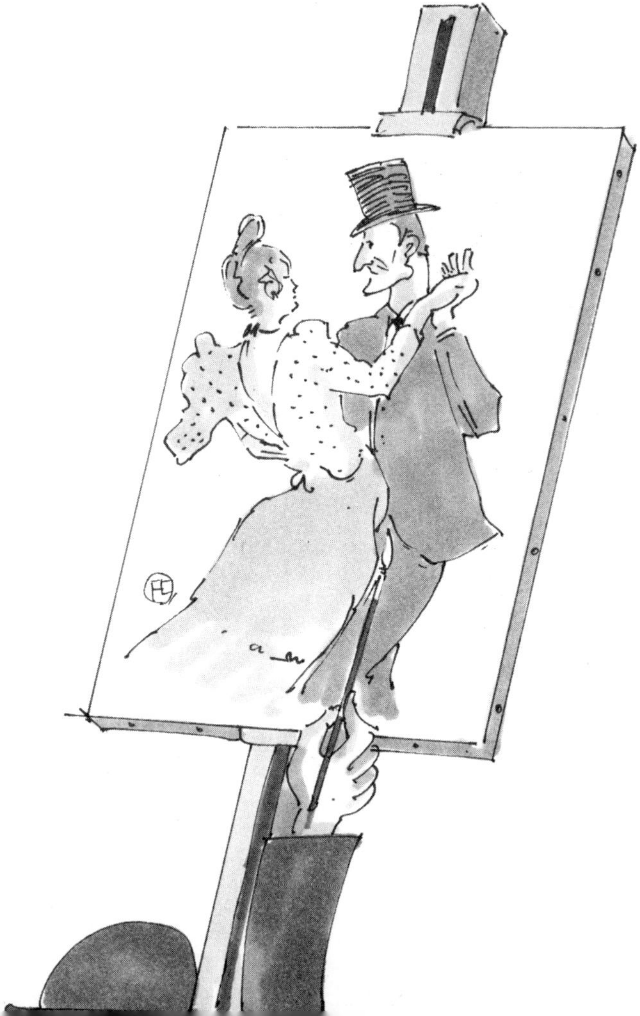

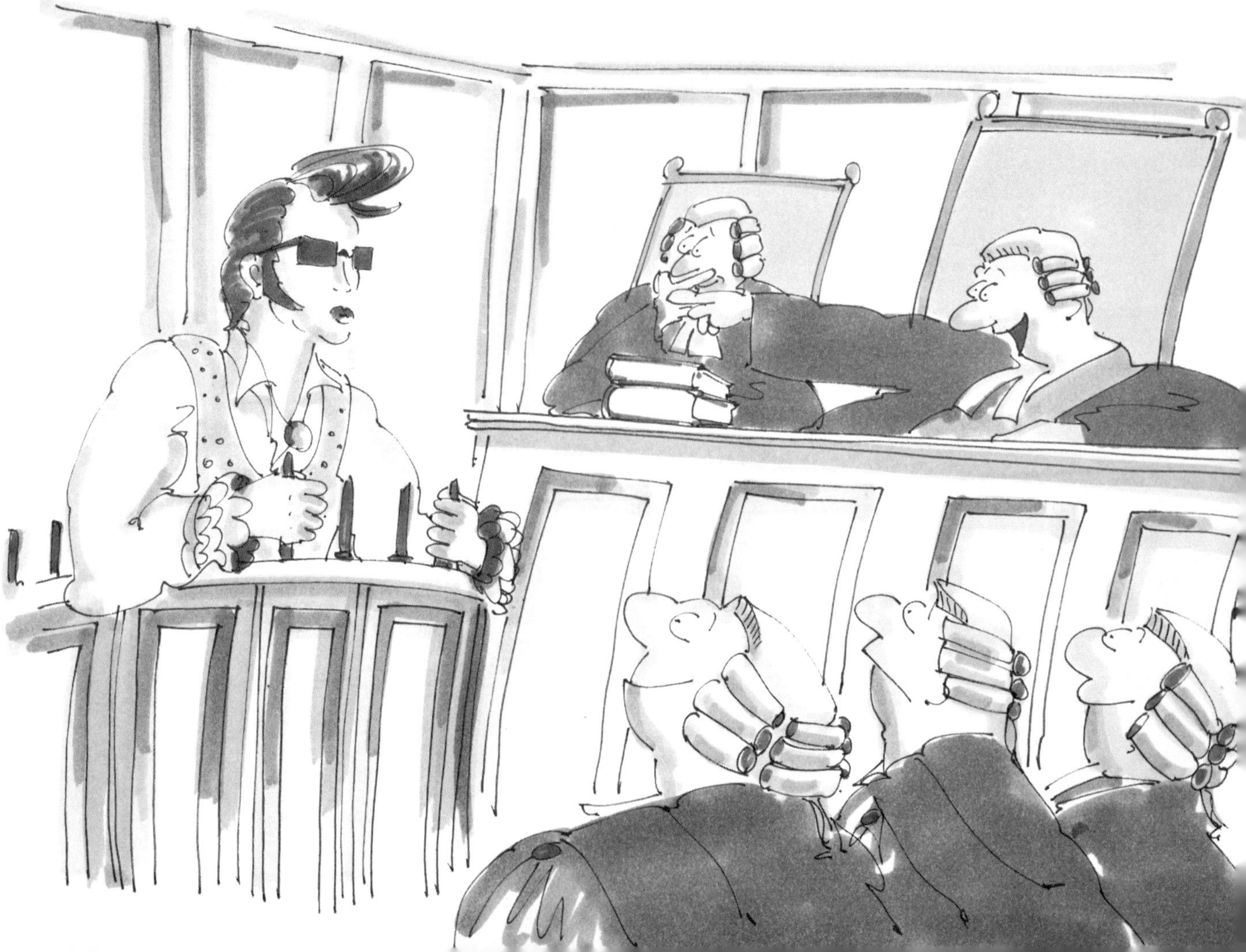

RETURN TO ZENDA

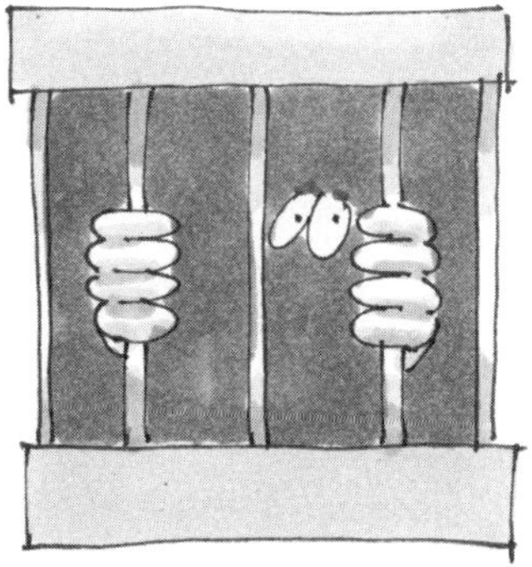

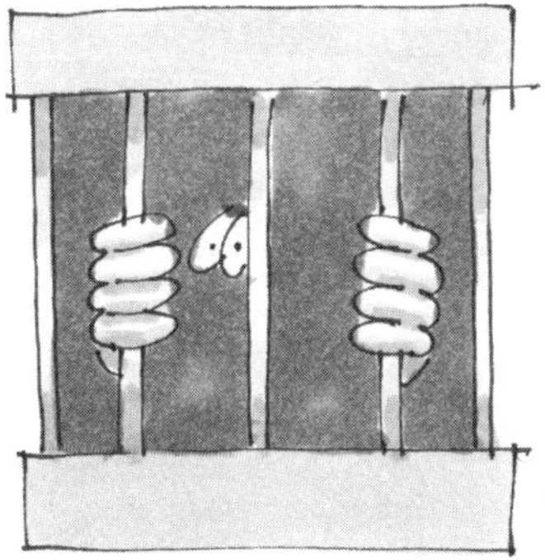

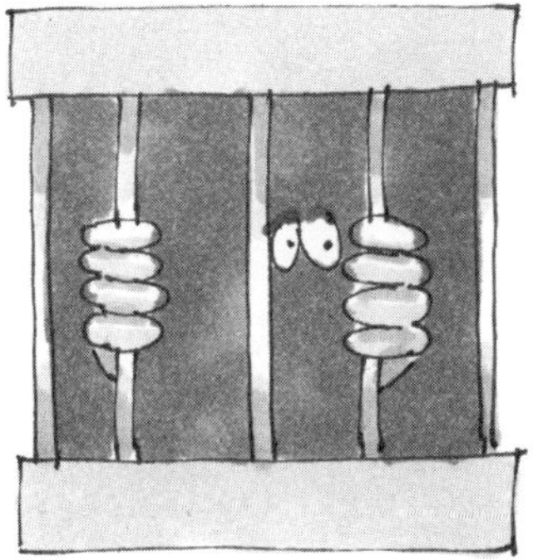

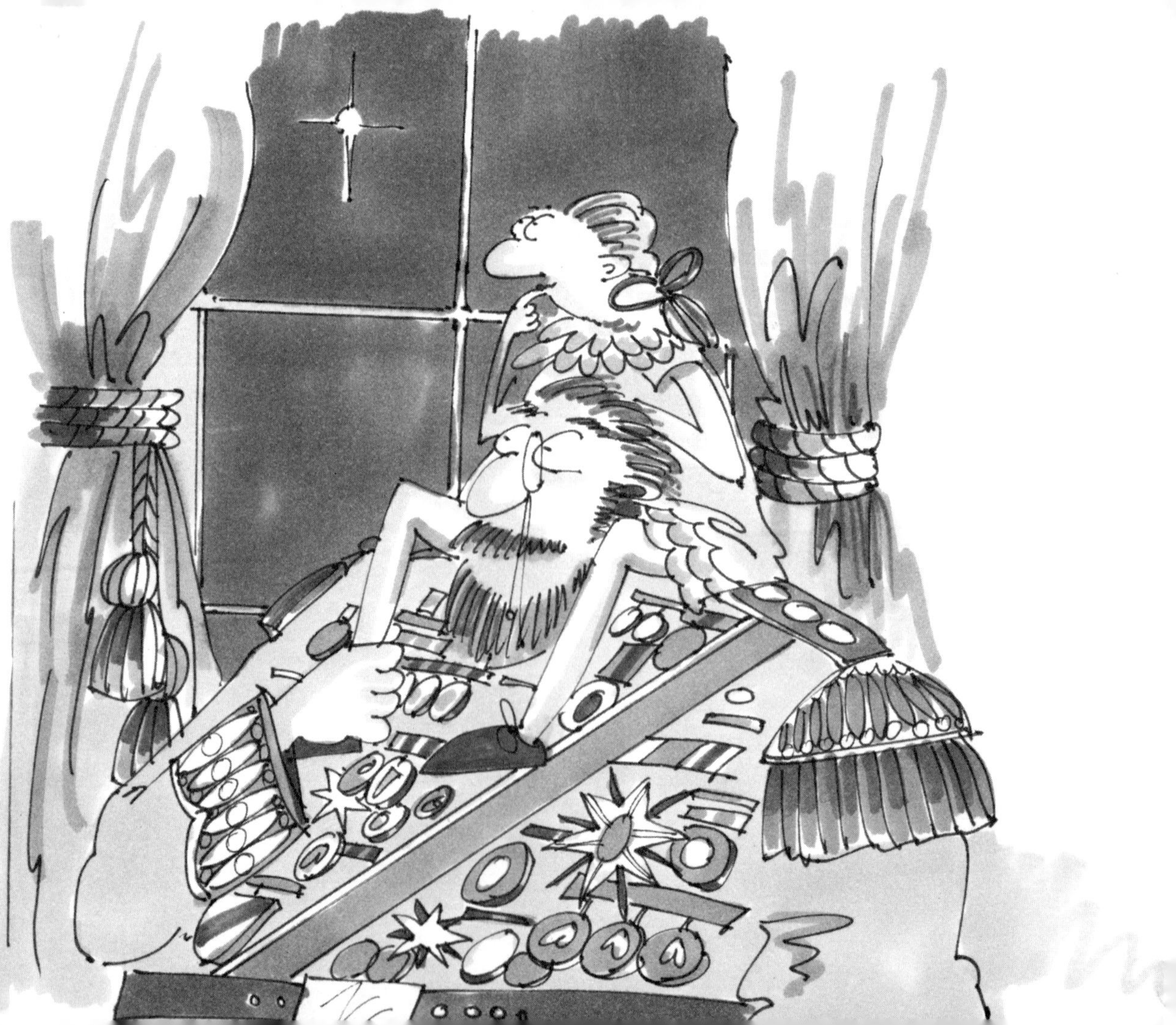

WHEN YOU WISH UPON A CZAR

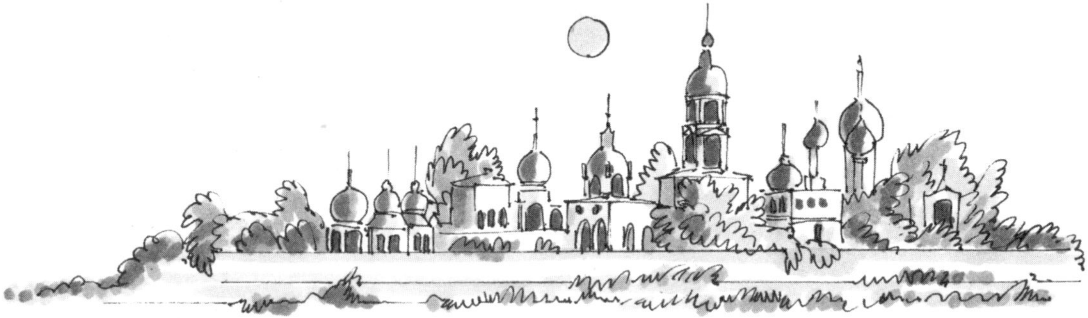

DISCOGRAPHY

Jailhouse Rock	Elvis Presley	1958
Never Mind The Bollocks Here's The Sex Pistols	The Sex Pistols	1977
Wherever I Lay My Hat That's My Home	Paul Young	1982
Jumping Jack Flash	The Rolling Stones	1968
Sailing	Rod Stewart	1975
Give Peace A Chance	John Lennon & Yoko Ono	1968
The Times They Are A-Changing	Bob Dylan	1964
Puff The Magic Dragon	Peter, Paul & Mary	1963
Doctor, Doctor	The Thomson Twins	1984
The Hills Are Alive With The Sound Of Music	Julie Andrews	1965
Send In The Clowns	Judy Collins	1975
Surf City	Jan & Dean	1963
Nights In White Satin	Moody Blues	1968
Wake Me Up Before You Go Go	Wham!	1984
My Way	Frank Sinatra	1969
Singing The Blues	Guy Mitchell	1956

Too Young	Nat King Cole	1951
I Shot The Sheriff	Eric Clapton	1974
A Day In The Life	The Beatles	1967
The Rivers Of Babylon	Boney M	1978
There's A Kind Of Hush	Herman's Hermits	1967
Lucille	Little Richard	1956
Hello Dolly	Louis Armstrong	1964
The In Crowd	Ramsey Louis Trio	1965
Words	F.R.David	1982
My Guy	Mary Wells	1964
Rocky Mountain High	John Denver	1972
Riders In The Sky	Ramrods	1961
Get A Job	The Silhouettes	1958
The Kids Are Alright	The Who	1966
Don't Mess With My Toot Toot	Denise Lasalle	1985
He Ain't Heavy He's My Brother	The Hollies	1969
I Only Have Eyes For You	Art Garfunkel	1975
The Dark Side Of The Moon	Pink Floyd	1973
The Loco-Motion	Little Eva	1962

Putting On The Ritz	Fred Astaire in Blue Skies	1946
When Two Tribes Go To War	Frankie Goes To Hollywood	1984
Begin The Beguine	Julio Iglesias	1981
Yesterday	Paul McCartney	1965
My Sweet Lord	George Harrison	1970
King Of The Road	Roger Miller	1965
Hello Mary Lou	Ricky Nelson	1961
Big Spender	Shirley Bassey	1967
American Pie	Don McLean	1972
We'll Meet Again	Vera Lynn	1939/45
Rudolph The Red Nosed Reindeer	Johnny Marks	1949
Spanish Eyes	Al Martino	1970
Ballin' The Jack	Chicago Footwarmers	1952
Hey, Hey We're The Monkees	The Monkees	1967
Born To Lose	Ray Charles	1962
Return To Sender	Elvis Presley	1962
When You Wish Upon A Star	Jiminy Cricket	1940